Sept 14, 1970

11 - 84615

*The Transformation of
American Foreign Policy*

Charles E. Bohlen

THE
TRANSFORMATION
OF
AMERICAN
FOREIGN
POLICY

W · W · NORTON & COMPANY · INC ·
New York

This book is based upon and is an expansion of lectures delivered at Columbia University by The Honorable Charles E. Bohlen in April 1969. This was the second in a series of Jacob Blaustein Lectures in International Relations sponsored by the Jacob and Hilda Blaustein Foundation in connection with the program of the School of International Affairs at Columbia University. These lectures are an expression of the intentions of the donors to make available to a wide audience the views of distinguished statesmen and scholars on major world issues of our times. Mr. Blaustein's high interest in international affairs has been amply recognized in his appointment by five Presidents to important missions in the international field, as well as in his membership in the United States Delegation to the General Assembly of the United Nations.

This book is of necessity more a summary of selected items and views than a history of the period.

Contents

I

The Transformation of American Foreign Policy

It is not possible within the space of these short essays to cover in any detail the vast and complicated aspects and effects of the transformation of the American world-role as the result of World War II and its aftermath. The author attempts here to deal only with what, to him, seemed to be the major causes and a few of the effects—notably, in regard to Soviet-American relations.

THE SECOND WORLD WAR made a tremendous impact on American foreign policy, and it followed that the years 1947–48, the years of decision, provided the basis of what now is our foreign policy and world role. But first of all, consider the historical tradition: the United States for over 150 years had lived under the admonition contained in George Washington's farewell address in September, 1796, in which he warned the people of the United States to beware of involvement in European affairs.

He said specifically, among other things, that Europe has a set of primary interests which have no, or a very remote, relation to us. Furthermore, he questioned the logic of interweaving our destiny with any sort of European entanglement. Our peace and prosperity, he said, could not be served as party to the toils of European ambitions, rivalries, interests, humor, or caprice.

The United States has faithfully and even religiously

followed the precepts of George Washington, but most of these were directed towards relations with Europe and the European continent. This is no accident, because at that time, 1776, with the exception of Japan and China, there were by modern definition almost no other "nations" in the world besides those in Europe. But in any case, until World War I, the United States had rigorously adhered to Washington's essential isolationism in regard to Europe. We entered World War I at a late date. We fought it as a foreign war; we returned. And the United States Senate rejected President Wilson's attempt to have the United States take the world position many thought proper—even necessary—in view of the nation's manpower, natural resources, trade requirements, and the simple fact of a geographical location which had become "central." As a result of Wilson's attempt to have the United States emerge from the cocoon of self-imposed isolationism and recognize its place in the world, there was a national reflex action which during the 20s and 30s, almost until the outbreak of the Second World War, produced a strong reaffirmation of non-involvement in the minds of the American people.

When the New Deal came into being in 1933, it was, as are all reform movements, inward-looking and uninterested in foreign affairs. An illustration was the rather brusque manner in which President Roosevelt in 1933 virtually broke up the London monetary conference by refusing, entirely because of domestic considerations, to be associated in the plans of currency stabilization. But towards the latter part of the 30s, the American government became increasingly concerned with what was going on in the world. There was first of all the rise of Hitler in 1933 and the extent of his increasing ambition; there was Mussolini's postwar Fascist takeover in Italy, and although we were slow in giving it our national attention, there was an imperial militaristic policy gaining strength in Japan. Roosevelt, in early October 1937, thought he would set out what might be termed a trial balloon in his quarantine speech in Chicago. He said that he thought it might be a good idea for the peaceful nations of the world to quarantine an aggressor, just as a community would act to quarantine the bearers of an infectious disease. The implications of this speech were that collective sanctions of a trade or other nature should be applied. The reaction to this suggestion was very quick and very negative on the parts of both Democrats and Republicans. At the time, I was on the way to the seven-power conference in Brussels which was to deal with the problem of Japanese aggression in Manchuria against China, and the uproar that greeted Roosevelt's remarks in 1937 was a clear indication to me that the United States was still strongly isolationist and that neither the people nor their Congress would tolerate any U.S. involvement in world affairs.

In fact, it was during 1935 to 1937 that the widely prohibitive Neutrality Act was passed. The supply of arms was rigorously controlled; the supply of arms by private individuals to belligerents in the event of war was not permitted. Even travel by Americans on belligerent ships was forbidden in the event of war. We went about as far as we could go in a complete policy of neutrality. In addition, there was the Ludlow Amendment, which provided for a national referendum before war could be declared. It was defeated in 1938 by only 21 votes in the House of Representatives.

I think all this indicates the extent of the tradition of non-involvement in the United States. Earlier—when I joined the Foreign Service on March 1, 1929—the United States had had about as safe, secure, and easy a position as any great nation on the face of the earth. We had neighbors to the north and south of us who constituted no conceivable threat. We were protected by two wide oceans, which in those days meant that no foreign nation could reach us. To the south we had Latin America, where we had relations that were on the whole friendly and even protective in continental terms. But more importantly, vast areas of the world were held by the two democracies who had been allied with the United States in World War I, namely, England and France. The British Empire in 1928—indeed it remained in the same condition up to World War II —controlled and administered an area of some thirteen million square miles. The population of that empire was 485 million. France also controlled large sections of Africa. In fact, on the continent of Africa there were only two significant nations that could be called even reasonably independent—the Union of South Africa and Egypt—and their relationship to the British Empire was close, although not exactly comfortable. France and England had been our allies in World War I and in general shared the philosophy held by the United States in regard to the organization of human society and the relation of man to society. At the end of the 1920s we were totally protected, and we acted accordingly.

The United States in those days was a non-military nation. The total budget of the United States was under four billion dollars in 1929 and 1930; the military budget for the United States was under a billion dollars; the budget of the State Department was approximately fourteen million dollars. Even if these figures are doubled in terms of "real value" of the dollar, they are nothing compared to what we see now. But, in any case, the United States had no military establishment to speak of; we had no commitments, political or military, to any independent country in the world. The only obligations, if you wish to call them that, that the United

States had on its books were the Monroe Doctrine, announced in 1823 (a very negative doctrine too—in a sense a warning to the Europeans that no new trespassing on the Western Hemisphere would be permitted), and the border treaties with Canada and Mexico; the treaties ending the Spanish-American War; and some involvement with the Open Door policy in China. The Monroe Doctrine was almost never put to a test. It was very vague and did not contain any concrete obligation on the part of the United States. We were really living in a completely protected, safe world.

As the 1930s moved to their close and we came closer and closer to world war, American policy began, to some extent, to move with the times and to depart somewhat from the neutral basis which we had laid down for ourselves. During this period, moreover, it should be noted, President Roosevelt moved to correct what he regarded as an anomaly in international relations; I think, also, he had in mind the necessity of taking some move to counter the aggression the Japanese Empire was pursuing at that time. The recognition of the Soviet Government, with which we had had no relations since 1918, was, at least indirectly and in part, motivated by concern in the U.S. government over this aggression by Japan in Asia, and the beginning of the rise of Hitler in Germany. Cordell Hull, in a memorandum to President Roosevelt in September, 1933, made specific reference to the Japanese situation as a factor favoring the recognition of the Soviet Union, and members of the Soviet Government made repeated reference to Japan in the early days in Moscow. In 1933 President Roosevelt invited Maxim Litvinov, the Soviet Foreign Commissar, to come to Washington, where they negotiated the conditions which underlay the eventual recognition by the United States of the Soviet Union. (More of this in Chapter III.) It is known that Roosevelt felt no stability could be achieved so long as we failed to recognize the existence of a nation of such potential.

Public opinion polls in the United States continued throughout the 30s to be very definitely isolationist. One Roper Poll taken in September 1939 showed that only 2.5 percent of the people polled were in favor of any form of intervention in the war then going on in Europe, while 30 percent were totally isolationist.

But it was obvious in the late 30s that the New Deal was abandoning its inward-looking posture in regard to Europe and was becoming more and more concerned at the rise of the dictators and at the darkening international scene. Roosevelt's quarantine speech in October 1937 was symptomatic of this trend. After the actual outbreak of the war on September 1, 1939, the administration was able to move off center and begin the pursuit of a much more active pro-Allied policy. The deal to provide destroyers to Great Britain; the Lend-Lease

Act, which could hardly be considered neutral; and the dispatch of American naval units to the North Atlantic with instructions to shoot in self-defense were all indicative of this trend.

An indication of the strength of the isolationist sentiment in the United States can be found in a campaign speech of President Roosevelt which he found necessary to make in Boston, Massachusetts, on October 30, 1940. He said then, "I have said this before but I shall say it again and again and again, your boys are not going to be sent into any foreign war." This statement was objected to by many of his associates, particularly Harry Hopkins, who told me during the war that he had been one of those who had strongly opposed the President's making it in an electoral speech. In Hopkins's opinion it was too risky politically and would soon be contradicted by facts which would tend to show the President of the United States to be a liar. Events proved the correctness of Hopkins's view. But there is a good deal of evidence that at that time President Roosevelt thought The United States would, if necessary, be able to intervene in the war through air and naval power alone. In any event, this particular pledge was indeed soon to be belied by the facts.

When the Nazis attacked the Soviet Union, Harry Hopkins was sent to Moscow for the first serious talk, I think, that any American had ever had with Stalin up to then. We had had two ambassadors, Ambassador Bullitt and Ambassador Joseph Davies, who had also seen Stalin, but there had been no serious or frank conversations. Considering the Soviet situation in July 1941, it is not surprising that Stalin talked frankly to Harry Hopkins about the military situation and the urgent need of the Soviet Union for American material help. As a result, Stalin's talk with Hopkins was almost totally devoid of the usual propaganda overtures which had characterized previous and subsequent Soviet conversations with foreign officials. Stalin gave a somber picture of the realities of the Soviet situation. But, at the same time, he did convince Hopkins that the Soviets would weather the attack. Hopkins's report when he came back from Moscow, expressing confidence in the Soviet Union's ability to resist, had a great deal to do with the determination of the United States to extend lend-lease assistance to the Soviet Union.

Then, of course, came Pearl Harbor.

I was, at the time of the Pearl Harbor attack, stationed in the United States Embassy in Japan. I recall that when the United States imposed economic sanctions following the Japanese move into Indochina in July 1941, it seemed to us in the Embassy perfectly clear that Japan would have to either fight or radically alter its policies; and it was rather clear, I think, to anyone who had even a remote knowledge of the Japanese character at that time that they would choose to fight. I recall a telegram Ambassador Grew sent to Washington during that period, in which he warned Washington not to expect from the American Embassy in Tokyo any warning of a Japanese military attack. He pointed out that the Japanese tradition had been to attack first and declare war later. Ambassador Grew undoubtedly had in mind the manner in which the Japanese had gone to war in 1904—first a naval attack at Port Arthur, then the declaration of war. As any such attack would probably be planned and prepared in a place far distant from Tokyo, the United States Embassy could not be expected to provide any warning. The attack came without warning at Pearl Harbor in 1941, and we were in the war.

It is worthwhile to emphasize the significance of a decision made by President Roosevelt that had a profound and vital effect on the future course of world history. He had decided to give priority to the European theater over the Pacific. President Roosevelt's position was supported by the Joint Chiefs of Staff. There was, however, considerable opposition to this decision within the American government, particularly in naval circles, and of course citizenry of the west coast held a different view. The decision was made possible by the fact that the Nazis, for some reason which only they could explain, rushed to declare war on the United States. Without the Nazi declaration, it would not have been possible for Roosevelt to give priority to Europe, and our main effort would have been concentrated in the Pacific. The consequences would have been far-reaching. The war in Europe would certainly have been lengthened, if not lost.

In general, the United States during the war years did not display any great departure from our traditional foreign policy. We fought the war to win the war. We paid less attention than we should have to the possible consequences, to what kinds of problems we would be facing at the end of the war, to what sort of political matters would require our attention. During this period, I was in Washington from 1942 on. At that time the United States military had a key voice, since military policy was the primary matter before us—and they had a larger voice in the conduct of all American affairs than they did later. As I have said, we fought the war to win it, and we would not allow political considerations to deflect us very often from this central aim.

In a sense the war years, rather than resulting in a sharp break from the isolationist past, can be seen as sort of a detour on the road. Many people in the United States foresaw a repetition of what had happened after World War I: that we would fight the war and then come back to roughly the same kind of world we had left, and everything would be splendid. It of course did not turn out that way. The American entry into the war changed very profoundly our relations with the two leading Allied powers—Great Britain and the Soviet Union.* President Roosevelt, through an exchange of messages with the "Former Naval Person" had established an intimate relationship which greatly facilitated our dealings with Great Britain following our entry into the war. With the Soviet Union, however, there had been no contact except the Harry Hopkins visit of July 1941, and Roosevelt was very anxious to meet Stalin. President Roosevelt, from the beginning of the Soviet-American wartime association, attempted to deal directly with Stalin. In December 1941 the President sent his first message to Stalin to try to arrange a "summit meeting" of the three leaders—Churchill, Stalin and himself. (In fact, Churchill went in on his own to Russia in 1942 and again in 1944.)

There was always difficulty in establishing face-to-face meetings, because Stalin maintained, possibly with sincerity, that his direction of military affairs in the Soviet Union was so determinant that he could not afford to leave Russia. It was not until November 1943 that a meeting was finally arranged in the Iranian capital of Teheran. Roosevelt and Churchill had proposed

---

* Despite the use of "Allied Powers", the United States was never formally allied with either Great Britain or the Soviet Union.

many other sites—Cairo, Asmara, Basra—but Stalin was adamant in saying that he could not go to any place which was not under Soviet communications control; so the conference took place in Teheran.

This was primarily, in fact almost exclusively, a military conference. There the decisions for the meshing of military plans were made, and the United States and Great Britain agreed that they would undertake the invasion of Western Europe "during May 1944" (although it turned out to be in the beginning of June). Winston Churchill was on the whole very reluctant to fix a date for the actual invasion. He kept saying that the date should be made conditional upon the state of Germany's defenses and preparations. Churchill's ambivalence as to the exact date of the invasion led, I remember, to a rather acrimonious accusation by Stalin, at one of the dinners, that Churchill had secret sympathies for the Germans. Stalin obviously did this as a means of expressing his irritation and concern at the Prime Minister's reluctance to fix a definite date for the overseas attack. I was personally disturbed to see that Churchill did not respond to these rather outrageous charges against himself, the man who had first led his nation in military resistance to the Nazis. Instead of either treating it as a joke (the whole thing was presented by Stalin in a semi-jocular vein) or getting angry and asking Stalin how he had the nerve to make such as accusation when the Soviets themselves had been in close harmony and association with the Nazis up until the time of the Nazi attack in June 1941, Churchill took a rather plaintive tone and said he didn't understand why Marshal Stalin was accusing him of such attitudes.

There was another incident at the same dinner which has been written up to some extent by certain American historians. Stalin remarked that, in his opinion, the only way to prevent the resurgence of German militarism would be to destroy the German General Staff. This would mean, he said, executing out of hand fifty to a hundred thousand members of the General Staff. Churchill took this remark quite seriously and immediately said that England could not go along with anything of this kind. The execution of enemies in cold blood, he said, was not in the British tradition. The President said that he would offer a compromise and proposed that they should execute forty-nine thousand. This has been used as an example of Roosevelt's desire to "appease" the Russians. Such a charge is perfectly ridiculous, since the exchanges were of no real importance and obviously made as a joke.

Subsequently, I believe (though I am not supported by historical documentation), Roosevelt sent Harry Hopkins to see Churchill, and Hopkins told him that the United States, ever since the Quebec Conference, in

August 1943, had been determined to fix a specific date for the invasion of France and that Churchill was just getting nowhere if he continued this evasive line. In any event, Churchill finally yielded; and, as was very characteristic of the man, once he had yielded, he became publicly a wholehearted supporter of the plan. I would say offhand that the Teheran Conferences were probably the high-water mark of Soviet-Western cooperation.

Up until a certain moment in the Teheran Conference, political problems had been only touched on. But then, in the discussion of Poland, President Roosevelt had told Stalin that because of the election coming up in 1944 (and I think this is the first intimation I had that Roosevelt was planning to run), he could not take any position on any Polish question. Stalin, while he probably didn't understand the vagaries of the American political system, seemed to agree, and he did not press the President. I never saw the slightest evidence that Stalin attempted to take advantage of the internal political considerations which the President voiced to him.

In any event, the military agreements reached at Teheran were carried out in a very exemplary fashion by both sides. The Allies landed on June 6, 1944. In making what must have been one of the greatest decisions ever taken by any single man, General Eisenhower alone decided, in the face of rather uncertain weather reports, to proceed with the invasion. One can imagine what would have happened if the weather had worsened during the night and those landing craft carrying American and British troops had crashed on the beaches of Normandy!

The Soviets faithfully kept their part of the bargain and launched their offensive in time to be of real help to the Allies. But there was one incident at the time which I believe accurately reflects the attitude of the Soviet Union to the Western Allies. Suddenly, after Teheran, in January 1944, there came a TASS report from Cairo to the effect that the British and the Germans had been meeting secretly in the Spanish Pyrenees. It was extraordinary to produce this report after what had, on the whole, been a relatively harmonious conference—especially in view of the fact that there *wasn't* any TASS correspondent in Cairo. The whole incident had been dictated by Moscow, a Cairo dateline put on it. I have never been able to find out what caused the Soviet government to produce this extremely and apparently unnecessary anti-British maneuver.

The next time the three leaders met was at Yalta. In view of its importance, I am devoting a separate chapter to this conference.

I I

The Yalta Conference

I KNOW OF NO CONFERENCE that has been so misrepresented or so misunderstood as Yalta. At Yalta, the final military plans for the defeat of Germany were drawn up. In addition, Yalta was the first time the United States and Great Britain, on the one hand, and the Soviet Union, on the other, had had to deal with political questions.

The Yalta Conference was not arranged without the usual difficulties as to a place of meeting. At this time, however, both Franklin Roosevelt and Winston Churchill realized that there was no chance of moving Stalin from his determination to stay within the area of Soviet-controlled communications with Moscow and, after a few suggestions which were turned down, did not argue the point, accepting Yalta on the Crimean Peninsula. In many respects it was highly inconvenient. As President, Roosevelt had a constitutional problem, since he was required to act within ten days on any piece of legislation adopted by Congress. Therefore, he could not be farther than five days' distance from the United States. Churchill at one point remarked that it was difficult to think of a worse place for the conference if one had searched the entire surface of the globe.

There was some conversation about the date, and originally the Yalta Conference had been projected in the minds of both Churchill and Roosevelt for November 1944. The 1944 election made it impossible for the President to meet that date. It was agreed, finally, that the meeting would take place in the beginning of February 1945.

The delay of the conference produced a very curious and interesting situation. Churchill had been in the United States visiting Roosevelt at the Quebec Conference in October and had subsequently gone down to Hyde Park, where he spent a weekend with the President. One day I was sitting in my office when Harry Hopkins telephoned and asked that I come immediately to the White House. Hopkins told me that he had held up a message from the President of the United States to Winston Churchill in regard to the latter's forthcoming visit to Moscow. In his incoming message to the President, Churchill had stated that, in view of the delay in the conference, he and Eden had felt it essential to initiate conversations with the Soviet Union, particularly on the subject of the problems of the Balkans. He added, however, that since he had just conferred with the President, he felt he knew his mind sufficiently well so that he could speak for both of them. Hopkins saw immediately in this a very serious threat to any postwar plans which the United States had in mind. He asked me what I thought about it. I told him that I thought that this would take out of our hands and turn over to the British the entire range of decisions which might have a determinate effect on the ultimate postwar situation in Eastern and other parts of Europe. Hopkins agreed, and together we sat down and drew up a message to Stalin and another to Churchill. In both messages, it was pointed out that while the President had no objections whatsoever to a meeting between Churchill and Stalin, even though he could not be present, he nevertheless wished to remind both of them that there was absolutely no problem in the world in which the United States did not have an interest as a result of this global war. He therefore asked them to bear this in mind and not to attempt to commit the United States in his absence to any important decisions. He also requested that Averell Harriman, our Ambassador to the Soviet Union, be permitted to sit in on the meetings so that he could be kept reliably informed. He concluded by saying that he looked forward to their meeting early the next year. The reaction to these two messages was intriguing. Stalin replied, saying he was very much interested to receive the President's message, since it gave a somewhat different slant on things than he had understood from Churchill's message proposing the meeting, but he was very grateful to the President for enlightening him. No reply was received from Churchill. It was during this visit of Churchill to Moscow during the autumn of 1944 that a number of things of considerable importance to the postwar world occurred. The first was an attempt at a Polish settlement which failed. Mikolajczyk was present (Mikolajczyk was then Prime Minister of Poland), and it must be admitted he was bullied by Stalin, and to some extent by Churchill, in an endeavor to get a settlement of Poland's frontiers and the cooperation of the government. The Russian demands were so excessive that Mikolajczyk felt no Polish Prime Minister could possibly accept them and remain in office. So this meeting ended in total failure, and the Polish frontiers remained to plague the Western Allies at Yalta.

The second point that was discussed during this visit —although this came to us only more or less indirectly later on—was the curious arrangement between Stalin and Churchill over spheres of influence. For reasons which totally escaped me at the time and have since, Churchill suggested that they make a percentage division of the degree of interest for each side in the Balkan countries. For example, in Greece, Britain was to be admitted to have ninety percent interest and the Soviets ten percent. In Yugoslavia, it was fifty-fifty. In Rumania, it was ninety percent Soviet and ten percent British, and in Bulgaria it was seventy-five percent Soviet and twenty-five percent others, in Hungary fifty percent Soviet, fifty percent others. While this unusual agreement will not be found in any British telegraphic traffic, I was reliably informed afterward from a British official who was in the Balkan area that they all received telegrams setting forth this division as an agreement by His Majesty's government. There is historical precedent: the Russians and the British had split up Persia in 1907, dividing the country by a physical line over which the other country could not pass. But to divide a country on a percentage basis is almost like saying that someone should be eighty percent or twenty percent pregnant. The Declaration of Liberated Europe adopted subsequently at Yalta certainly was contrary to any spirit of such a naked spheres-of-influence agreement as Churchill proposed to Stalin on the back of an envelope in Moscow in the fall of 1944.

The preparations for Yalta must have been very difficult for the Soviets, but the Soviets were the ones, of course, who were most keen to have the conference on Soviet soil. It was necessary to transfer down to Yalta the equipment of three entire Moscow hotels. Absolutely nothing had been left in the Crimea or in the palaces that had been set aside for the visitors. The Germans had taken out even such things as doorknobs, steps, window fastenings—in fact everything. There were only the bare buildings left. The Soviets set up perfectly comfortable quarters, particularly in the Lavadia Palace, where Roosevelt was to stay, and where the main meetings were to be held.

It is obviously not possible in this summary to describe all the proceedings of the conference that lasted eleven days and which has been the object of study and intense scrutiny by subsequent historians and statesmen, many of whom had axes to grind. I will therefore try and give in summary form the results of the conversations in some of the discussions. Let me start out by saying that there were two errors made by the United States alone.

The first of these mistakes was the Soviet-American agreement in regard to the Far East. There was, however, a reason which at the time appeared valid to President Roosevelt: both at Malta and later at Yalta the chiefs-of-staff of Great Britain and the United States had jointly informed President Roosevelt and Winston Churchill that the war in the Pacific would last eighteen months after the end of hostilities in Europe. At that time, two American operations—Coronet and Olympic —were far along in the planning stages, and they would have involved the transfer of the bulk of the American army from Europe to the Far East for an assault on the

Japanese islands sometime in the fall of 1945. It had been estimated by the American military that it would cost about 200,000 more in American casualties to assault the Japanese islands before rather than after Soviet entry into the Pacific war. I doubt if any American President in our history—or in the future—would be insensitive to such advice; it is inconceivable that any President would not have adopted a decision preventing 200,000 American casualties. Therefore, Roosevelt accepted what Stalin termed Soviet desiderata in connection with the war in the Pacific. These were the return to the Soviet Union of territory which had been taken from Russia by the Japanese after the end of the 1904 war—Southern Sakhalin and the Kurile Islands. Here again we see a case where lack of precision was so important to future events. "Kurile Islands" were the words used in the Yalta agreement (without qualification). Actually, following the Russian-Japanese War of 1904, the Japanese annexed the entire string of Kurile Islands, but the two southern islands had never been Russian. Nevertheless, since the term Kurile Islands (without qualification) was used in the agreement, the Soviet Union gave it the broadest possible interpretation and literally occupied and stole, if you will, two islands from Japan. The Yalta Agreement also provided for certain economic facilities and positions for the Soviets in Manchuria and the Port of Dairen.

It is worth noting that this arrangement was made by Stalin *not* in any expectation of a Communist takeover of China. This is shown by the fact that once Mao Tsetung became the boss of China, the first thing he did was to go to Moscow in 1950 and arrange for the annulment of these agreements by the Soviet Union. The arrangements in the Far East agreed to by Roosevelt were, in the words of Talleyrand, "worse than a crime, they were an error," since they were based on a faulty estimate of the length and of the course of the war against Japan. They were unpleasant and immoral, especially in that the Manchurian Port of Dairen deal involved arrangements for the territory of a de facto ally behind the back of its government. The reason for this was the certainty in the minds of the American and Soviet officials that anything told to Chungking would end up in the hands of Tokyo within a matter of days. In any event, this was certainly a mistake, although I personally doubt whether the map of Asia in the immediate postwar period would have been any different; and it is worth mentioning that the Soviet-Chinese treaty which was signed in the early summer of 1945, and based on the Yalta Agreement, was on the whole hailed by the press in this country, as well as elsewhere, as a great step for the consolidation of peace and stability in the Far East.

The second mistake at Yalta was the deal over the voting in the United Nations. President Roosevelt was very much impressed by the difficulties which President Wilson had encountered with the United States Senate over the question of multiple voting in his attempt to have the United States join the League of Nations. He had with him on this delegation two men who had been very active in Washington at that time. One was Ed Flynn, a Democratic Party official from the Bronx; and the other Jimmy Byrnes, subsequently Secretary of State. I gather that these two men told Roosevelt it would be a mistake to provide the Soviet Union with more votes than the United States had. It should be recalled that at this time the Soviets had proposed the initial admission of two of their constituent republics— White Russia and the Ukraine. Largely because of the British insistence that India must be an initial member, although it had no independent status in 1945 (this was to come later in 1947), Churchill therefore supported very strongly the Soviet request when it was made at Yalta, stating that his heart bled for the sufferings of these great republics, who, in his opinion, were more entitled to consideration as initial members than many of the other nations which had been proposed. Churchill had in mind, of course, some of the South American countries, who had not really been participants in the war. Because of the advice that President Roosevelt received in regard to possible opposition in the Senate to any arrangement involving multiple voting in the

United Nations, he sought and obtained from Stalin a letter which promised that the United States would have three votes to match the Soviet three votes in the General Assembly of the United Nations. This, later on, unfortunately leaked in Washington and was the subject of an outraged cry of protest on the part of American political and public opinion. It was not so much the fact that the two Soviet republics had been admitted to the United Nations General Assembly, although this in itself seemed to be hardly necessary; it was really what looked like trickery, with the United States receiving three votes in return. I do not know how President Roosevelt would have handled this, but from the very slight knowledge I have of his methods, it was quite possible that at the San Francisco Conference which he had planned to attend, he would have withdrawn the request for three votes once the reaction had been known.

Aside from these two errors, there were a number of agreements reached at Yalta, none of which can be termed a success, but none of which can be attributed with reason to mistakes or weakness on the part of the Western Allies. The first of these was the problem of Poland, concerning which an endeavor was made to set up a composite government that was supposed to submit itself to free elections. Also there was the agreement in regard to the Polish-Soviet frontier, which was to run roughly along the Curzon line in Eastern Poland, with the Western frontier of Poland left open for the ultimate peace conference. Poland was the subject which probably caused the longest, most tedious, and most frustrating debates with the Soviet Union at Yalta. The result was far from satisfactory to anyone present on the Western side, but in stark truth there was nothing else that could be done. Roosevelt, before Yalta, had endeavored, without success, to obtain Soviet concurrence to withhold Soviet recognition of the puppet government of Poland organized in the Soviet Union. He endeavored also to have the city of Lwów left to the Polish side of the frontier, again without success. But one other aspect of the Yalta agreement on Poland should, I believe, be mentioned; I have not seen it referred to in any history book. During a visit I paid to London with Harry Hopkins in early 1945, I saw the Polish Prime Minister Mikolajczyk. At that time Mikolajczyk and I discussed in detail and depth the entire problem of Poland and what we would face at the Yalta Conference, which was coming up in the next week. Mikolajczyk made one point very strongly. He said that one thing the Western powers should not do under any circumstances was to withdraw, as it were, the hem of their garment and leave Poland alone to the tender mercies of the Soviet Union. He pointed out that the Western Allies had very little leverage in the Soviet

Union at this particular juncture. He recognized that the whole of Poland was occupied by the Red army, but, he said, "you must make the best deal you can, the best arrangement, the one that will give the best opportunity to safeguard the liberties of the Polish people, but do not, in discussing these agreements, *do not* abandon that country completely." The letter President Roosevelt sent Stalin at Yalta, listing the names of a number of prominent Poles from which the leaders of a Polish Provisional Government could be selected, was based on a suggestion from Mikolajczyk. The Western Allies also made an effort to have the Soviets accept the idea that ambassadors Harriman of the United States and Clark Kerr of the United Kingdom were, together with Molotov, to have general supervision over the Polish election. This Stalin fought and fought successfully, using the time-worn cliché that was often in the Soviets' mouths when it suited their interest: that to impose any supervision over a country would be an insult to (Polish) national pride. In any event, the Polish agreement was made. It seemed at the time (and still does to me) the best agreement that could have been made. But it must be understood that the totalitarian state is impervious to the regular, ordinary means of pressure which sometimes are available between countries. Since a totalitarian government has no private entities or institutions that operate in the commercial or business field, there is very little that can be done to affect its decisions, short of outright force or the threat of force, which obviously we were not proposing to do at the time.

Another agreement at Yalta concerned the Declaration on Liberated Europe. This was spelled out in a document prepared in the Department of State that set forth principles on which the three powers would be guided on any matters connected with the internal or external affairs of enemy countries to be occupied by the Allies. There was to be consultation and joint agreement as to how the situation was to be handled. I have never understood why the Soviets accepted this with so little argument. But, in any case, they did so, and the fact that they did refutes the idea, heard from time to time, that the United States and the British made at Yalta a "spheres of influence" agreement with the Soviet Union on Europe. Such an agreement was not made in any form, shape, or manner. The Declaration on Liberated Europe is the exact antithesis of any spheres of influence agreement in Europe, since it provides for the participation of all three major Allies in any of these matters dealing with occupied countries.*

One other point I would like to touch on is the question of zonal boundaries in Germany. It has often been said that the zonal boundaries were really finally approved by the three governments at Yalta. This is not true. The zonal boundaries were approved by the gov-

---

* The validity of any of the Stalin-Churchill discussions in October 1944 on percentage degree of influence in the Balkans remains unclear.

ernments on November 14, 1944. At Yalta the matter was never discussed by the Big Three at the conference. The only aspect of zonal agreement that *was* discussed was the granting to the French Republic of a zone of occupation for Germany, which was to come out of the British and American zones.

The subject of France, incidentally, played an important point in this conference. Churchill was the strongest proponent for France at the conference. He argued cogently and intelligently that it was impossible to envisage the future of Europe without, as he put it, a "lively France." He also strongly supported the idea that France should be given a zone in Germany and should, furthermore, have a full and equal seat on the Control Council. President Roosevelt agreed with the idea of giving a zone to France but hesitated a good deal about granting them a permanent seat on the Control Council. He felt that the inclusion of France would only lead to trouble and bitterness and difficulty. It must be remembered that at this time de Gaulle was causing a good deal of trouble to the Allied side. Stalin, moreover, was virtually adamant on the subject of France. He got up and walked up and down behind his chair, a sure sign that he was deeply interested in the question under discussion. He said that France was rotten; that Pétain represented the real France and de Gaulle only the imaginary France; that France had opened the front to the enemy and had no more claim to be represented with the big victorious powers than many other countries who had fought better. He named specifically—and ironically enough in light of future events—Yugoslavia, pointing out that Yugoslavia had had as many, if not more, divisions fighting against the Germans as France had been able to furnish after 1940. Finally, Roosevelt said he wished to think of the matter overnight, and that evening after the conference, Harry Hopkins, H. Freeman Matthews (who was head of the Western European division of the Department of State), and I called on the President and urged him to agree to have France a member of the Control Council, pointing out that it was quite anomalous to have a country administering a zone of Germany without sitting on the major body of direction and control. We also pointed out that, since it had been decided at the conference to invite France to participate in the declaration of liberated Europe, it was quite inconsistent to exclude her from taking part in the Control Council for Germany. The following day at the Conference, Roosevelt said that he had thought this matter over and had finally come to the conclusion that, on balance, it was better to give France a seat on the Control Council. At this point Stalin raised his arms in a gesture of surrender and said, *"Sdaiyus,"* which in Russian means "I give up."

There were many other matters discussed at Yalta, none of which were of exceptional importance.

During this conference, there were many amusing and

important examples of Soviet attitudes towards the West that came out at the dinners and luncheons with which all conferences are replete. Although Roosevelt was not a well man at Yalta and certainly did not have his normal degree of energy and health, I do not know of any case where he really gave away anything to the Soviets because of this ill health. He seemed to be guided very heavily by his advisers and took no step independently. I might add here another point which has been made much of during the Joseph R. McCarthy period in the United States: the charge that Alger Hiss had been one of his most intimate advisers. This was not true. Alger Hiss was at Yalta for United Nations affairs, and he stuck very closely to this line of work. He never saw Roosevelt alone in the entire course of the conference. I know this because, as Roosevelt's personal interpreter, I had to be standing by the President at all times, in order to be available should there be an unexpected meeting between him and Stalin.

Another issue, which appeared at the time to be important but in actual fact had very little to do with the treatment of Germany, was the Soviet insistence of fixing a sum of reparations in the amount of twenty billion dollars, some of which was to come from current production. The British, with vivid memories of the fiasco of reparations at the end of World War I whereby the victorious Allies ended by paying a great deal of Germany's reparations to themselves via credits and other loans, were adamant in their opposition to this proposal. The President apparently did not feel quite so strongly and, under the promptings of Harry Hopkins, finally agreed to have the subject (that is, the twenty billion dollars in reparations) scheduled for further discussion at the forthcoming meeting of the reparations experts in Moscow. Churchill resisted even the discussion of such reparations, and with reason, in my opinion; he was very much disturbed when the United States did not join with him. In fact, I recall, during the intermission toward the end of one of the conferences, Churchill came up to me with his lighted cigar. With a glowering face, he poked me in the stomach and said, "Young man, no matter what position we occupy here, we will be judged by history, and we will be severely judged if we have turned Germany into a sinkhole of poverty and misery."

It was at the Yalta Conference that Churchill coined one of his most brilliant alliterative phrases, but it was due to a misunderstanding. Churchill had not had his normal afternoon nap, because he had lunched with the President, and he arrived at the four o'clock meeting feeling a little out of sorts and possibly a little exhilarated, although not noticeably so. He misunderstood a report that Secretary Stettinius was making at the Foreign Ministers Meeting in the morning, and thought that Stettinius was proposing to put the British Empire under trusteeship. Even though Eden was trying to tell him that this was not the case, Churchill announced belligerently, "We will never tolerate the fumbling fingers of fifty nations prying into our heritage." Eden was finally able to break through, and the remark was never translated, much to the relief of the British interpreter.

The Yalta Conference was the first time the Western democracies and the Soviet Union had come to grips with the political problems which would follow the war —problems relating to frontiers and to political systems. President Roosevelt considered Yalta a trial of the ability of the West to work with the Soviet Union. It was indeed a trial, and the verdict was soon forthcoming. Yalta showed the total incompatability between the ideas of the Soviet Union, ideologically motivated by the doctrines of Karl Marx, and the Western democracies. The democracies by their very nature do not adhere to any one single ideological system. The Soviets did and felt it to be their duty as Marxists and internationalists to introduce or even impose their system whenever this was possible without undue risk to the Soviet Union.

It cannot be said that Yalta was a success, but, as I wrote earlier, there are no grounds for supposing that it was the folly or the weakness of the Western powers which made this true. The map of Europe would look exactly the same as it does today if there had never been a Yalta Conference.

46

I I I

Soviet-American Relations, 1808 to 1946 — A Review

A T THE TIME of the Yalta Conference in early 1945, in fact for months before that time, there was undoubtedly a considerable degree of illusion in American thinking on relations with the Soviet Union. There was also an unwarranted optimism in regard to the future role of the United Nations in world affairs. Even before the end of the war, a good reflection of current American thinking on the postwar issue can be found in a statement made by Cordell Hull before the Congress on November 18, 1943, following his return from the Moscow Conference of Foreign Ministers. In referring to the four-power declaration adopted at Moscow which forecast the formation of the United Nations, Mr. Hull told the Congress, "as the provisions of the four nations' declaration are carried into effect, there will no longer be need for spheres of influence, for alliances, for balance of power, or any other of the separate alliances through which in the unhappy past the nations strove to safeguard their security or promote their interest." This was, I believe, the prevailing opinion in the American government all through the war and up to 1947.

Before I discuss postwar Soviet-American relations, it is important to review, quickly, the relationship between the two countries which originated early in the nineteenth century. Russian-American relations began in 1808 when the Czar's government, the last of the great powers to do so, established diplomatic relations with the young American republic. By an ironic twist of history, the United States over a century later was to be the last of the great powers to recognize the Soviet republic. It is an historical fact that from the moment of the establishment of relations, there were no conflicts, indeed no major causes of friction, between the United States of America and the Russian Empire. At one point in 1814, the Czarist government at our request sought to act as the mediator between the United States and Great Britain in the War of 1812. There was even an amusing suggestion by some of the Czar's diplomats in 1827 that it might not be a bad idea for the United States to maintain some naval units in the Mediterranean. And during the Civil War, the Czar displayed a sympathetic attitude toward the Federal government and the Union cause. In 1863 Russia sent two naval squadrons on visits

of friendship to the United States—one to San Francisco
and one to New York. And finally, in 1867, we were able
to purchase Alaska for the ridiculous sum of $5,800,000.
These incidents are merely cited as indicative of the fact
that the two countries had no major conflict of interest,
no major territorial dispute between them, and therefore
no cause of conflict. These amicable and harmonious
relations persisted up until the beginning of the twen-
tieth century when the great influx of Russian im-
migrants, many of them refugees from the oppression
of the Czar, began to change the climate of American-
Russian relations. The Kishenev massacres in the early
part of the century and the vigorous United States public condemnation of them reflected this mood. Nevertheless, from the early part of the nineteenth century up
until World War II, two of the great countries of the
world were able to live together without any serious conflict. I mention this truth because it underlines an important element in our relations with Russia. Even now
there is really no conflict of interest between the United
States as a country and the Soviet Union as a country.
The tension between us is, in my opinion, caused by the
ideological factor.

In March 1917 occurred what, I believe, most historians would agree was the real Russian Revolution.
It was a spontaneous uprising of the Russian people be-

ginning in Petrograd against the Czarist regime. Among the many reasons for it were the war-weariness of the Russian people, the repeated failure and shattering losses of the Russian army in the war, the breakdown of the supply system, and the failure to provide food to the populations of the cities—particularly in Petrograd. All these contributed to a situation in which, without the directing force of any revolutionary organization, the people rose up in March and overthrew the Czarist regime. The United States immediately—the day after its establishment—recognized the Provisional government which emerged out of this revolution. (It is important to remember this fact, in view of the widely accepted belief that, after her own, the United States became historically allergic to revolution per se.)

In the summer of 1917 we sent a mission headed by Elihu Root to examine conditions in Russia and find out what the United States could do to assist. It must be said that the report of the Root mission was perhaps not the most prescient in the world, since it did not remotely envisage the possibility of the overthrow of the Provisional government. It is worth remembering, however, that the United States had excellent and allied relations with the revolutionary Provisional government of Russia. Then, of course, on November 7, 1917, came the Bolshevik seizure of power. I use the term *seizure of power* rather than *revolution* because this is what it was. It was a seizure of power by an armed minority in the city of Petrograd, followed by the seizure of power in various Russian cities. At no time in the early days of their rule did the Soviet government—the Bolshevik government, as they called themselves then—have any majority support.

The United States during this period took a very critical attitude toward the new Soviet regime, as did all the Allied governments. The initial reason was that the Soviet government had decided to seek a separate peace with imperial Germany at a time when the Allies, particularly late in the spring of 1918, were under heavy pressure from the German army. Given the temper of the times, it was understandable that the United States, Great Britain, and France, the chief Allied powers, did not take a very lenient and sympathetic view towards a revolutionary government which had set as its first aim the conclusion of a separate peace, allowing the release of German troops from the Eastern front for use in the great and critical German offenses in the spring of 1918.

The first document of the Soviet republic, which was issued on November 8, 1917 (the Decree of Peace, as it was called), contained—and this is important for future historical reference—the two elements that have intertwined in Soviet foreign policy since that time. The first was a relatively normal diplomatic appeal to the Allied governments for the conclusion of an immediate peace. The second, in the same document, was a strong appeal to the revolutionary proletariat, as they saw it, of all the world to rise up and overthrow their governments. This dichotomy between state-to-state relations and revolutionary theory was to reflect itself in varying degrees in the future. As a result of the particular philosophy of the Soviet government installed by the *coup d'état,* to give it its correct name, in 1917, the United States did not maintain diplomatic relations with it. In 1918 our ambassador was withdrawn from the Soviet Union, and from 1918 to 1933 the United States had no official relations with the Soviet Union. The other countries of the world, particularly the major powers, eventually recognized the Soviet Union, mostly in 1924 and 1925. But the United States held out, largely, I think, through certain principles which were expressed by Secretary Bainbridge Colby in August 1920 to the Italian government. Colby outlined the reasons the United States did not recognize the Soviet Union. They were, in effect, that the United States thought the Bolsheviki, by their announced principles and policies, were violating all the accepted norms of international intercourse; that they were engaged in encouraging, subsidizing, and directing revolutionary movements against virtually all governments in the world; and that they had repudiated the debts of their predecessors. This view remained that of the United States government until 1933, when, as already noted, President Roosevelt decided to establish diplomatic relations with the Soviet Union.

Maxim Litvinov came to the United States in November 1933 to undertake negotiations looking towards the re-establishment of relations. There were three substantive agreements, not of equal importance. The first and most important one was the apparent renunciation by the Soviet government of its support and direction of revolutionary activities against the government of the United States. President Roosevelt and William C. Bullitt, about to be our first ambassador to Moscow, thought that they had achieved a genuine agreement with the Soviet Union on this important question. The second point of some importance was the agreement by the Soviet Union to negotiate for the repayment of the debt of monies loaned by the United States to the Provisional government of Russia. And the third, which was relatively less important, was the granting of religious rights of Americans living in Russia. At that time, of course, the attitude of the Soviet government was very strongly anti-religious, and they permitted no churches or any religious entities to operate on their soil.

William C. Bullitt was appointed by President Roosevelt to be the first United States Ambassador to the Soviet Union. The choice appeared logical. Bullitt had been sent to Moscow in 1919 by the Peace Conference in Paris. He had had intimate conferences with Lenin and had come out with a favorable impression of the Soviet regime in Russia. Bullitt, in setting up the Embassy in 1934, anticipated finding a comparable regime.

It did not take very long for Bullitt to be disillusioned. He found Stalin's Russia—and by 1934 it was indeed Stalin's Russia—to be very different from the Russia he had known in 1919. The informality of the early Bolsheviki and the frankness of their talk had been replaced by a totalitarian structure founded on suspicion and concealment. On the debt question, the Soviets claimed that we had offered them a loan—technically that term had been used in the communiqué following Litvinov's visit. But taken in context, it clearly meant we referred to a credit. The Russians clung to the technical interpretation of a loan, which meant that money was to be loaned from one country to another without any strings attached to it, whereas a credit must be spent in the country making the credit available. This was the first illustration brought home to American diplomats of the importance of precision in dealing with the Soviet Union and of leaving nothing to chance or to the generalized belief in the good faith of your partner. Bullitt found also that the agreements which he had made with Litvinov were not to be honored. The Soviet government, as was its practice, refused to accept any responsibility for the activities of the Communist International, which held a meeting in Moscow in 1935. This led, on Bullitt's recommendation, to the exchange of some bad-tempered notes between the two governments. It was not long before these and other disappointments produced a very marked change in the attitude of Ambassador Bullitt, who was for the rest of his life a consistent and at times violent opponent of the Soviet Union. He felt, and very strongly, that Litvinov had reached freely negotiated agreements with President Roosevelt and with himself, and that the violation of them by the Soviet government or its avoidance of the assumed obligation through technicalities were acts of bad faith which precluded any form of good or even normal relations between the United States and the Soviet Union.

If Ambassador Bullitt found the Russia of 1934 very different from the Russia of 1919, for anyone who has experienced the Soviet Union since that time, the Soviet Union of 1934 was in the opposite sense a very different country from what it subsequently became. It was possible then for members of the American Embassy to have relatively easy non-official contacts (and I use the term "relatively" very often in describing the Soviet

Union, because nothing is absolute in that country except the Communist Party), with many members of Soviet society, particularly the theatrical people, artists, and even some official people. I recall one dinner that Ambassador Bullitt gave at the Embassy residence during the summer of 1934 at which he had Bukharin, Karl Radek and a Soviet journalist called Mikhailski, who wrote for *Izvestia* on American affairs. There was a conversation during that dinner which I have never forgotten. Karl Radek said to me in Russian, in commenting on some remark made by Ambassador Bullitt, "You Westerners will never understand Bolshevism. You consider Bolshevism as a hot bath whose temperature can be raised and lowered to suit the taste of the bather. This is not true. You are either 100 percent in the bath and 100 percent for it, or you are 100 percent outside and 100 percent against it." I have seen this remark of Karl Radek's borne out time and time again in dealings with the Soviets.

1934 was a year of optimism in Russia. The famine of the early 30s, a by-product of collectivization, was over, and there was considerable hope among the population that a certain measure of freedom was to be introduced into the Soviet Union, largely on the grounds that the revolution was over and had triumphed.

Another conversation of that period was indicative of

Soviet thought in 1934. In July 1934 the Soviet government officially changed the name of the secret police from OGPU to the People's Commissariat of Internal Affairs or NKVD. On the day of this announcement, Litvinov told Bullitt that he would venture to predict that the term NKVD would hold no more terror for the average Soviet citizen than the name of the New York Police Force for the citizens of New York. This is certainly one of the most massive misstatements that history knows, for it was precisely the NKVD which carried out the terrible purges of the late 30s. The murder on December 1, 1934, in Leningrad, of Sergei Korov, member of the Politburo and Party Chief of that city, has generally been recognized as the signal which led in the next few years to the unleashing of the most terrible purges in modern history in any country. It was the purges that in many ways set the pattern of the Soviet Union as we have known it since and as we know it today.

There is little to tell about Soviet-American relations for the period of 1934–1939. The purges affected all foreigners in Moscow and especially their relations with the Russian people, but the main foreign targets of the purges did not include the United States. Relations were distant and formal. Soviet-American relations, however, were seriously chilled by the Nazi-Soviet Pact concluded at the end of August, 1939, which was certainly the trigger, and was so intended to be, that set off World War II. The negotiation leading to this agreement had begun in the spring of 1939, but this short book is not the place to go into all the details of this extraordinary event. The visit of Ribbentrop, the Nazi Foreign Minister, to Moscow on August 23, 1939, burst on a startled and somber world. There the non-aggression pact between the Soviet Union and Nazi Germany was signed, despite the fact that in Moscow at that time were the British and French military and political missions which had been negotiating with the Soviet government, supposedly to obtain the Soviet adherence to the general Western Alliance against Nazi Germany.

Now, I think, a few words of explanation are needed about the reasons why, as it seemed to me at the time, the Soviet government decided to make this fateful agreement. Those who remember the occasion will recall the absolute stupefaction that hit almost every government and public opinion throughout the world at the announcement that Communist Russia and Nazi Germany had signed this pact. The American government had a source which kept us informed during the whole course of events, so the treaty was not a surprise to officials in Washington; but it certainly was to American public opinion. It seemed clear at that time that the aim of Stalin, who by then was the complete boss of the Soviet Union and sole source of policy, was to keep the Soviet Union out of war at all cost. It is interesting to note that the attitude of the Soviet Union towards the possible outbreak of European war seemed to vary with the distance of the locus of possible war from the Soviet frontiers. The nearer to the Soviet Union, the more cautious the Soviet attitude. When the theater of war was in Spain, the Soviets were very active and did not trouble to conceal their support and aid to the Spanish Republicans. Later on, when the theater was Czechoslovakia in 1938, the Soviets were still relatively bold and outspoken in their words, but much more cautious in regard to any commitment which might involve them in military action against the aggressor. When the scene shifted to Poland, a contiguous country, Stalin clearly saw that if the Germans attacked Poland without the benefit of some offsetting Nazi-Soviet deal, the chances were considerable that the Soviet Union would be drawn into the war. I consider this to be the major reason why the Soviet Union, in cold-blooded realistic appraisal of its chances, opted for the deal with the Nazis. It has always been the belief of Marxian ideology, engendered by Lenin, that capital had no country and that, all other things being equal, the capitalist countries would unite against the Soviet Union. This was a continuing Soviet nightmare. Like many aspects of Soviet ideological thought, this thesis was accompanied by an antithesis— that capitalist countries could not unite with each other because of their inherent rivalry and competition for markets. In 1939 Stalin foresaw a war among capitalist countries, namely Nazi Germany and the Western democracies, and sought to deflect it from Soviet soil. The Soviet government therefore abandoned any efforts toward collective security which they had followed since 1934 and made their deal with the Nazis. This cynical and cold-blooded switch on the part of the Soviet Union could not fail to have had a strong and deleterious effect on Soviet-American relations. The United States from the very beginning of the war was pro-Ally and anti-Nazi, and therefore the spectacle of the Soviet Union, heretofore the chief propaganda opponent of the Nazis, joining hands with Hitler was very keenly resented in the United States. Another event that most certainly served to chill relations even further was the Soviet attack on Finland in December 1939. Covered by their pact with the Nazis, the Soviets decided that they must bring about, in the interest of Soviet security, some adjustments in the Soviet-Finnish frontier. When diplomatic discussions failed to get anywhere, they launched an open attack. In so doing, they almost automatically increased their aims in regard to Finland; this increase became clear with the establishment of a completely bogus "Soviet" government at Terioki on the Soviet frontier. Illustrative of the general reaction of the American people were the words of President Roosevelt to a group of the representatives of the American Youth Congress—a Communist front organization—in the courtyard of the White House in February 1940. It was the first and, I believe, the only time that he had been booed and hissed by an audience as President of the United States. He said, "The Soviet Union, as everyone who has the courage to face the fact knows, is run by a dictatorship as absolute as any other dictatorship in the world. It has allied itself with another dictatorship, and it has invaded a neighbor so infinitesimally small that it could not, it could do no possible harm to the Soviet Union." This is, I would say, an accurate expression of the official and popular American attitude towards the Soviet Union during the war and up to June 1941 when the Nazis attacked without warning or provocation. From that moment on, the relationship between the United States and the Soviet Union immediately changed. In June 1941 Winston Churchill made a speech in which he said that he threw the full weight of the British Empire behind the Soviet Union in their war with Nazi Germany, while maintaining his position against Communism. A comparable statement was made by Acting Secretary of State Welles.

The interesting thing about these two statements is that they show a considerable degree of naïveté. The maintenance of this paradoxical position of supporting a country while disapproving its regime turned out to be totally impossible as the war went on. What happened was that the disapproval of the regime was submerged in the necessity of helping the country. And this became the characteristic American and British attitude toward the Soviet Union during the war. There was no way of controlling publicity favorable to the Soviet Union, even when it was implicitly pro-Communist, while our armies were fighting a common enemy.

I have noted earlier that Harry Hopkins met with Stalin shortly after the Nazi attack on the Soviet Union. It is known that his arduous and dangerous journey resulted in a firsthand and favorable estimate of Russia's chances of survival. Up to the time of Hopkins's visit to the USSR, both the American military and the British military had given the Soviet Union virtually no chance of survival against the Nazi army. Hopkins, after his visit, voiced the opposite opinion. Subsequently, U.S. Lend-Lease aid to the Soviets amounted to some eleven billion dollars in war materials. There was a mission headed by Averell Harriman and Lord Beaverbrook in September 1941 which formalized an agreement on the

Lend-Lease. Throughout the war, although American relations with the Soviet Union were correct in that no signs of strain were allowed to appear in the Soviet press—nor much in the United States press, relations were far from intimate, and on the whole rather formal and distant. In contrast to the situation in World War I, no Allied officer was permitted ever to visit the Soviet front. Liaison was conducted through Allied military missions, both British and American, in Moscow during the whole war; and there was no really intimate sharing of military strategic plans, although, from the military point of view, the Soviets behaved on the whole as a loyal ally and carried out accurately and on schedule their part of the military agreements as to the timing of offensives and comparable matters.

Nevertheless, there grew up, particularly in the Anglo-Saxon countries, which were the only allies then of the Soviet Union, a considerable amount of pro-Soviet sentiment. Some of it was based on the fact that the Russians were bearing the brunt of the war in Europe for the first two years or so following our entry. The Soviets were containing some two hundred and fifty or two hundred and sixty Axis divisions on the Eastern front, and we had not yet invaded Europe. Also, among the hangovers or relics of the isolationist atmosphere in which we had lived for our whole national existence was the belief that somehow evidence of good will was of paramount importance in international affairs. The Soviets had never displayed that particular quality in their international relations. So we often found ourselves in the position in which we seemed to be almost apologizing to the Soviets for existing at all, as well as for our "failure" to do more to help. The Western Allies never officially referred to the fact that the Soviet Union had been on the whole quasi-allied with Nazi Germany from 1939 until June of 1941. But certainly the record of the attempts on the part of the Western Allies to aid the Soviet Union is very impressive. A good illustration was the extraordinary difficulty and danger of the North Sea route where the convoys sailed into Murmansk with frightful losses. The Soviet attitude of suspicion and distrust of its allies was completely in conformity with the basic view engendered by Marxist-Leninist philosophy that capitalist countries must be regarded as being by their very nature hostile to the Soviet Union.

This failing of United States diplomacy—an over-eager desire to be agreeable in international relations—was well revealed during the visit of Molotov to Washington in June 1942. He came secretly to the United States under the pseudonym of Mr. Brown. During that period in Washington, he succeeded in getting the United States government to sign a communiqué which referred to the importance of the urgent task of setting up a second front in 1942. This was vigorously opposed by the Department of State on the grounds that it was misleading and would cause trouble later on. Most people in the American government at that time knew, I think, that it was not going to be possible to set up a trans-channel landing in 1942; but the White House and President Roosevelt thought that it was important to make a gesture towards the Soviets. Technically read, the language of the communiqué did not commit the United States to open a second front in 1942, but it certainly left that implication, and the Soviets made use of it.

This was not the first example of one of the deficiencies of American diplomacy, particularly in dealing with the Soviet Union—the absence of real precision. We have learned since then that any arrangement of any kind made with the Soviet Union must be precise and clear and not subject to different conscious interpretations. When, as noted, Winston Churchill went to Moscow in the summer of 1942 to explain to the Soviet leaders that it was not going to be possible to set up the invasion of Europe in 1942, it is known that he had a very rough time with Stalin. And we have seen that, in later meetings, Stalin was to accuse the British of everything from fear of, to collaboration with, the Germans.

Although I have touched on some of the significant aspects of the Teheran Conference in Chapter I, there is one aspect of that meeting which is worth elaborating upon here from the point of view of our foreign relations generally and our relations, specifically, with the Soviets. During that conference President Roosevelt outlined his view of the future world organization. Churchill had been rather inclined to the idea of a regional security council, and so had Stalin. Roosevelt explained to Stalin that he did not feel that this would be possible. Because of the isolationist sentiment in the United States, there was no chance that the American Congress or that the American people would support American involvement in a purely European body. I think that he genuinely succeeded in persuading Stalin that the only possibility of United States participation was in a world-wide body such as the Security Council which would be charged with the problems of maintaining the peace in the entire world. At least Stalin ended by agreeing with him. He also explained the idea of the General Assembly where each nation would have one vote; but the peace-keeping mechanism, according to President Roosevelt in 1943, would be the Security Council, in which he envisaged four or five great powers who would be the guardians of the peace and who would occupy strong points throughout the world, particularly in regard to Germany.

There was a slightly amusing incident at the time of Churchill's seventieth birthday dinner, which he gave at the British Embassy at Teheran on November 30, 1943. It was one of those dinners where the toasts were endless and innumerable. At one point, President Roosevelt made a toast to Sir Alan Brooke, the Chairman of the British Imperial Chief of Staff, on the basis that he had known Sir Alan's father, and that he was sure if Sir Alan's father were alive, he would be immensely proud of his son, and asked everyone to drink to Sir Alan's very good health. Everyone drank to this, but then Stalin rose to his feet and said that while he had drunk the toast, he would really like to express the hope that Sir Alan Brooke would become less suspicious of the Russians and would learn to trust them, since, Stalin said, the Russians were not bad people.

There was considerable consternation among the British guests after this toast because Sir Alan Brooke, an Irishman, was reputed to have a quick temper, and it was feared he would make a quick and intemperate reply to this seemingly gratuitous insult. Sir Alan remained silent for about fifteen minutes, and then arose and thanked the President and said he wished to comment on the remarks of Marshal Stalin. Sir Alan Brooke said the only reply he could make to Stalin's comments was that he had perhaps been fooled by the Soviet cover plan as it had existed from 1939 until the German attack in 1941. His remarks were particularly appropriate since the conference had been considering "cover plans" to deceive the Germans as to the actual place and time of the invasion of Normandy. Sir Alan had in fact told the Russians in polite but nonetheless pointed terms that it was too much to expect people at war with Nazi Germany to have a very high regard for the Soviets during the period of their association and alliance with Nazi Germany. Stalin took Sir Alan's remarks in good part and said he thought there was much to what Sir Alan had said.

After the Teheran Conference, the Western Allies concentrated their energies on mounting the landing in Normandy. As this invasion was a success, it removed the chief point of Soviet criticism of the Western wartime policy. The Normandy assault was backed up by a Soviet offensive. The military moves presented no problem in regard to our relations with the Soviet Union.

But on another level, the political level, from the time of the Yalta conference, relations between the United States and the Soviet Union deteriorated very rapidly. The Polish crisis was not solved by the agreement at Yalta. The Soviet Union chose to disregard some of its basic provisions and proceeded to go its own way in the setting up of a Communist regime in Poland, which led to a continuous acrimonious exchange of messages between the Soviet Union and the other two participants at Yalta. In Rumania, the Russians proceeded within less than a month of Yalta to violate one of the most important documents of the conference, the Declaration on Liberated Europe, which provided for three-power consultation on all issues involving the administration and control of enemy-occupied countries. They sent Vyshinsky down to Rumania to browbeat the Rumanian government into acceptance of what was to be the forerunner of the Communist government of Rumania.

Soviet-American relations were certainly not helped by disagreements which arose over the meeting set up in Switzerland to arrange for the surrender of the Germans in Italy. The United States, backed by Great Britain, properly felt that this was a matter for the Theater Commander, Lord Alexander, to handle in its initial phases. The general order to all military commanders in the entire Western front was for "unconditional surrender." It was felt that the presence of a Soviet representative at the preliminary meeting might complicate matters to the point where an opportunity to bring about the surrender of the Germans in Italy might be lost. The Soviets chose to interpret this decision of the Allies as an attempt by them to bring about a separate agreement with the Germans to end the fighting in the West while permitting it to go on in the East. In fact, Stalin in a message to President Roosevelt, dated April 3, 1945, made a flat charge to this effect. He accused President Roosevelt of not being fully informed on this matter. President Roosevelt was understandably incensed at the insulting nature of Stalin's accusation and sent back a very firm and frank message. I recall this incident very well, since I participated in the drafting of Roosevelt's reply. After explaining in some detail the essence of the matter involving possible German surrender in Italy, Roosevelt concluded with the following:

> *"Finally I would say this, it would be one of the great tragedies of history if at the very moment of the victory, now within our grasp, such distrust, such lack of faith should prejudice the entire undertaking after the colossal losses of life, materiel and treasure involved.*
>
> *"Frankly I cannot avoid a feeling of bitter resentment toward your informers, whoever they are,*

*for such vile misrepresentations of my actions or
those of my subordinates." ∗*

I saw at this time many evidences of President
Roosevelt's serious concern over the deterioration of
our relations with the Soviet Union. He had considered Yalta the test of the ability of the three powers
to resolve their differences and to work towards the
common purpose, namely, keeping the peace of the
world. He was profoundly disturbed by the evidences
of the Russian violation of the agreement on Poland
and the agreement covering the Balkan countries.

The original idea of the Soviets had been not to send
their Foreign Minister to San Francisco in April 1945,
and I think this is probably a genuine indication of the
doubts and lack of basic interest in the Soviet mind
about the United Nations. But after the death of
the President, Ambassador Harriman suggested to
Stalin that if the Soviet government wished to do
something to show the feeling of the country over the
loss of Roosevelt, the best thing in his view would be
to send Molotov to San Francisco. Stalin agreed to this,
and the United States, sent a special aircraft to
bring Molotov to the United States. On his way to

∗ See *Foreign Relations of the United States 1945,* Vol. III, pp. 742
and 746.

San Francisco, Molotov passed through Washington and had a meeting with President Truman, who had just recently taken office. I was Truman's interpreter at that particular meeting, which took place April 22, 1945, at the White House. During this interview President Truman was most insistent that the Soviet Union carry out the commitment Marshal Stalin had taken on himself at the Yalta Conference with regard to Poland and the countries of liberated Europe. Molotov replied with the usual Soviet maneuvers and even implied at one point that the United States was trying to impose its will on the Soviet Union. President Truman kept insisting that we were asking only that the Soviet Union carry out the Yalta decision on Poland. The interview ended with the President repeating that the United States government was prepared to carry out all the agreements reached at Yalta and he asked that the Soviet Union do the same. President Truman repeated this assertion in a message he sent to the Soviets on the same day. The President terminated the interview by handing Molotov a copy of a proposed press release of their meeting.

At this time, however, the French Communist Jacques Duclos published his historic article in the *Cahiers du Communism* (April 1945), in which he attacked Earl Browder for his decision to dissolve the

American Communist Party and transform it into a political association. Duclos, in opposing Browder's action, pointed out that the United States was still a class country, that we had "trusts" which had fascist elements, and that therefore to abandon the purpose of class warfare was to abandon Marxist-Leninist ideology. In other words, this was a reaffirmation of the classic principles of Marxism which had always been and still are an obstacle to normal relations between the Soviet Union and other countries throughout Soviet history.

On February 9, 1946, in an "election" speech made in Moscow, Stalin asserted that, after all, the war was caused by the uneven development of capitalism—he cited Lenin to that effect—and that there was no reason to believe that, as long as capitalism existed, one could really make a world that would be free of the threat of war. He called for an immense Soviet effort to rebuild the country and develop its national economy for its own security, ie., security against attack by the capitalist nations.

These, I feel, were the origins of the cold war as it involved the United States, though the full weight of the crisis was not recognized until the next year. The reasons the Soviets acted as they did is perfectly clear. They were still convinced of the correctness and infallibility of the doctrines of Karl Marx and, even more so, of those of Lenin. For the sake of relations with the Western Allies, these views had had to be muted during the war. There had thus been a period of some four or five years when the Soviet people had not been made aware of the continued ideological faith of their rulers. It is very likely that Stalin and his associates were fearful that the Russians were coming to believe that the Soviet leaders were no longer Marxists-Leninists. And those who say that it was Churchill's Fulton speech in March 1946 which was the real beginning of the cold war are, I think, misstating the case. Here it is appropriate to consider the basic elements of cold war, elements without which I don't believe that it is possible for any nation to initiate such war.

First, there must be an overriding absolutist philosophy or ideology. Secondly, there must be a totalitarian system of government which controls every single outlet affecting public opinion: press, radio, television, spoken or written word. In questions of abuse of opponents, there was a definite Bolshevik tradition. The Russian Bolsheviki from the very beginning had never pulled any punches in the denunciation of an adversary, regardless of whether this adversary had been an old friend or not. Recently, for example, in Soviet broadcasts for April 1, 1969, in English directed to the Far East, the statement was made that Mao Tse-tung in 1945 had said to an important American visitor that it was wrong to believe that great men were those who had done the most for humanity. Great men, according to Mao, were those who had shed the most blood. That is literally what the Soviet broadcast said. It went on to assert that now, during the civil war in China, Mao had decided it was cheaper to recruit new members for the Chinese Communist Armed Forces than it was to take care of the wounded, and that as a result there were hundreds of thousands of Chinese who had been wounded on the Communist side during the civil war who had been allowed to die on the battlefield. I merely cite these things as examples of what you might call cold-war techniques, which, beginning certainly no later than 1947, were to be applied intermittently to the United States and still are.

Churchill's speech in Fulton in March 1946 was only a public statement of a whole series of truths in regard to the situation in Eastern Europe and the actions of the Soviet Union, of which every government was aware, but which had not been articulated, for reasons of maintaining good relations with a former ally. Churchill had the courage to say the truth, and he said it in the United States.

The first public conflict between the United States and the Soviet Union in the postwar period occurred over the Iranian Case in March 1946. During the war in 1941, the British and Soviets had jointly occupied the Territory of Iran. The purpose was to prevent the Axis use and infiltration of Iranian territory, which was a vital link at the time in the line of supply to the Soviet Union. The agreement with the Iranian government provided for the withdrawal of the troops within six months after the end of hostilities. The Soviet Union chose to interpret this to mean not the end of the war in Europe but the end of the war in the Pacific, which came some three months later. It became apparent at the end of 1945 that the Soviet Union did not intend to honor this treaty. It was the subject of discussion between Secretary Byrnes and Marshall Stalin in December 1945, and it came up briefly before the first meeting of the Security Council in January 1946. It became an issue between the United States and the Soviet Union in a session of the Security Council in March 1946. At that time, largely because of the American attitude, the Soviets yielded the point and agreed to withdraw their troops from Iran. This was one case in which the United Nations, without any use of force or threat of force, was able to achieve an important political victory. There was one aftermath of this event which I recall very vividly. It took place at a small dinner in Paris given by Mr. Byrnes for Molotov in April 1946.

Molotov complained to Byrnes over the United State's attitude in the Iranian case before the Security Council, saying that he thought that it was most extraordinary behavior on the part of an ally and friend to have taken issue with the Soviet Union for a trivial offense such as overstaying the treaty limits and keeping their troops in Iran. He said, in effect, what are a few thousand troops in a small country like Iran? What difference does it make among friends? He thought that the great powers should not interfere with each other in what they were doing in bordering countries. In fact, I think he mentioned in this connection that had the United States decided to do the same thing in regard to Mexico, there would have been no reaction from the Soviet Union. It was a very clear expression of Bolshevik political morality or lack of morality.

Mr. Byrnes tried to point out to him that we were signatories to the Charter of the United Nations, which we had, indeed, been instrumental in bringing into being, and one couldn't sign something and then ignore the meaning of its provisions simply because of certain political necessities. This, I really think, was totally incomprehensible to Molotov. In any event, from about 1946 and 1947 on, the United States became public enemy number one and still is, in terms of Soviet propaganda output. Output has been raised and lowered and varies with certain circumstances, but by and large the Soviets have continued to treat the United States as the chief obstacle to the Soviet ambitions in the postwar world and consequently as Public Enemy Number One.

I V

_____

Years of Decision

1947 AND 1948 WERE, in my opinion, the years of decision as far as American foreign policy is concerned. They were the years in which we were forced to do things we had never intended to do, and had no thought of doing, and certainly really did not want to do from the point of view of the strict material interest of the United States of America.

As an example of the attitude of the United States and Great Britain in the postwar period, I will cite some statistics of the military strength of the Allied forces in Europe. At the end of hostilities on the continent of Europe there were something like five million armed men in the Western Alliance of Great Britain and the United States. The U.S. Army in Europe in 1945 numbered 3,100,000 men. The United Kingdom army was smaller, with 1,300,000. The United States reduced its forces in Europe from 3,000,000 down to 391,000. The United Kingdom went from 1,300,000 down to 299,000 and the Canadians, who had had 485,000 in Europe, had zero in 1946. This, of course, was the great year of demobilization of the American civilian army—which is what it was—and I think it is probably the greatest proof that can be given (some might call it naïveté) of the general innocence of American intentions at that time.

At the Council of Foreign Ministers in 1946, the ministers dealt almost exclusively with the problems of the peace treaties of the satellite areas, the Balkans and Italy. The Soviets refused to consider the problem of Germany, taking advantage of the fact that the original draft of the Potsdam agreement had listed the Balkan countries and Italy ahead of Germany and using this sequence to postpone consideration of Germany until a later date. (Another example of the importance of precision.)

In February of 1947, the British Embassy came to the Department of State and said that the British could no longer continue their support of the governments of Greece and Turkey. Therefore, if there was to be any further assistance such as the British had supplied, it would have to be undertaken by the United States. This was the first overt intimation that the United States government had of the war's profound effect upon the strength of the British Empire. In fact, one of the most astounding features of the war and immediate postwar period was that literally no one in the American government foresaw the extent and rapidity of the decline of British power. I do not believe that Roosevelt thought of his anti-colonial attitude as a factor in Britain's decline. Here is an extraordinary twist of history. The American President morally opposed British imperialism yet counted upon the power of Great Britain (essentially powerful as the leader of a great Empire) as an equal democratic partner in the postwar world! President Roosevelt thought the British Empire would develop into a commonwealth of free nations which would not diminish Britain's overall power. In any case, from an Empire controlling 13 million square miles, with a population of 485 million, Great Britain was reduced in the space of a few years to a cluster of islands off the coast of Europe. The process of dissolution of the British Empire had already begun in 1947 when India was given her independence. Great Britain had stood alone against the might of Nazi Germany from June 1940 until June 1941. At this time the Soviet Union joined the struggle, not by her own will, but by the action of the Nazis. It was, at war's end, difficult to believe that this country which had put on such a magnificent war effort could really be headed for a decline of power which would change the whole international scene. Roosevelt was not alone in believing that at the end of the war there would be three great powers— Great Britain, the Soviet Union and the United States—two of them in the democratic column and one in the totalitarian column. All the great wartime conferences had been based on the existence of three great powers, and it was unthinkable, and indeed unthought of, that one of them would suffer so swift and radical a decline in power within a few years after the end of the war. Obviously the whole world was radically altered by the fact that Great Britain visibly could no longer continue to carry the burdens she had borne for so long in the past. It was in the face of such realization that the United States, in the person of President Truman, made probably the biggest decision for the future of American policy. He could have decided that Greece was a country remote from the United States, with no immediate lines of communication; that it was far on the other end of the Mediterranean; and that it was none of our business. He could have washed his hands of the whole thing or he could have done what he did. He picked up the challenge, and went to the Congress of the United States with the Greek-Turkish Act. I was in Paris at that time with General Marshall, on the way to Moscow. When we received the text of the President's message, we were somewhat startled to see the extent to which the anti-Communist element of this speech was stressed. Marshall sent back a message to President Truman questioning the wisdom of this presentation, saying he thought that Truman was overstating the case a bit. The reply came back that from all his contacts with the Senate, it was clear that this was the only way in which the measure could be passed. I think this, again, is a reflection of some of the isolationist thought that was still very prevalent in the United States.

It was not until 1947 that we had the first serious discussions about Germany with the Soviet Union. The Council of Foreign Ministers, which included the United States, the Soviet Union, Great Britain, France, and China (when the Council was dealing with Germany, China was not present, since she was not party to the German surrender instrument). The first meeting took place in Moscow in March and April 1947. This will always remain in my mind as a very important conference. The Soviets were extremely negative and would not agree to anything. When General Marshall went to call on Stalin on April 19, 1947, I went along as his interpreter and note-taker. He found Stalin in a very relaxed mood, saying, in effect, what difference does it make if we can't agree now; after all, we can come back in six months and try again, and even if we don't agree then, life will still go on. This attitude impressed General Marshall very much indeed. He talked about it all the way back to the Embassy and all the way back to Washington on the plane. General Marshall felt that Stalin was obviously waiting for Europe, harassed and torn by the war and in virtual ruins, to collapse and fall into the Communist orbit. Stalin, as Marshall saw it, seemed to think that it didn't make any difference to the present situation whether there was much recovery in Europe. By implication, sooner or later the Communist party would take over.

The impression made by Stalin on General Marshall was certainly one of the main causes of the Marshall Plan. From Moscow, Marshall set up the Policy Planning Staff, which was headed by George Kennan; and the first task he assigned to it was to draw up a plan for assistance to Europe. Shortly thereafter Will Clayton, who was then Assistant Secretary for Economic Affairs, returned from a trip to Europe and presented Marshall with a very interesting memorandum dealing with the "invisible" damages of the war, in which he pointed out that in addition to the physical damages which the war had caused the continent of Europe, there was a whole series of unseen damages—the breaking of connections of a business nature, insurance, shipping, and so on—all these had been disrupted and torn asunder. General Marshall bundled all these together with the first report of the Planning Staff. He sent them to me to prepare a first draft of a speech he was to make at the Harvard Commencement on June 6, 1947. I prepared the first draft of that address, adding a few thoughts of my own. The speech was reworked by Marshall himself before the final version. I mention the sequence leading up to the Harvard speech because there has been a tendency in some quarters to believe that General Marshall had really no idea what he was doing, and that he just stumbled into what turned out to be one of the great ventures of American postwar diplomacy. This, I can assert, is not true. His speech at Harvard was the direct result of the thoughts that he had begun to have in Moscow after seeing Stalin in 1946, and which were strengthened by his reading of Will Clayton's memorandum. He produced it at Harvard with full knowledge of what it meant. But he gave strict orders throughout the Department of State, particularly in the Press Section, that there was to be no publicity at all given to this speech. His reasoning was very clear on this. He felt that if the speech got a great deal of attention in the United States, it might arouse a storm of opposition in the Middle West. The taxpayers of the country on the whole were very conscious of the amount we had contributed to UNRRA. Marshall was, in effect, gambling that the Europeans would see the importance of his proposals and that the center of attention would be focused on Europe rather than on the United States. For this reason, he did not officially notify any European government, neither the British nor the French, of the intent of his Harvard speech. It is true, however, that Dean Acheson, the Under-Secretary of State, did talk to three British correspondents of the significance of Marshall's speech just prior to its delivery at Harvard. But in any case, it is to the eternal credit of Ernest Bevin, the British Foreign Secretary, that he recognized the importance of what had been said and immediately reacted. The result was a meeting between the French and the British, who both responded very favorably to the idea.

Then came a curious little interlude. A day or so after he had made the speech at Harvard, at a meeting in the Department of State, General Marshall turned to George Kennan and me and said, "I am going to get a question as to whether or not we would include Russia among the possible recipients of the offer that I outlined at Harvard." Marshall fully realized that if the Soviets did accept, it would be the end of the plan. He added, "On the other hand, if we don't include them, it obviously looks like an anti-Soviet measure and we'll lose a lot of support throughout the world." Kennan and I looked at each other and said we were convinced that the Soviet Union could not accept the plan if it retained its original form, because the basis of self-help and the fact that the United States was to have a voice with the receiving country as to how the aid was used would make it quite impossible for the Soviet Union to accept, given the nature of the Soviet structure, and particularly because of the political control which they were establishing over the countries of Eastern Europe. The historical record shows that the Soviets flirted with the idea of participation in the Marshall Plan; Molotov took a team of eighty to Paris in the summer of 1947 and talked to the French and the British. The Soviet version of what they should do was a very simple one. A shopping list should be drawn up and presented to the American government, which would then hand out the money very generously and would have nothing to do with how it was administered or spent. This was the Soviet idea, but the British and the French stood firm on the original Marshall Plan and refused this suggestion. However, the Czechs accepted the invitation to Paris, and the Poles made a half-hearted attempt to accept it. The treatment of the Czechs by Stalin was a forecast of future events in Czechoslovakia—summer of 1968. Stalin called the key members of the Czech government to the Kremlin and told them bluntly and brutally that if they went through with this, they would forefeit any pretense of friendship of the Soviet Union and the Soviet Union would know what measures to take to deal with the matter. The implication was perfectly clear. In retrospect, I think the Marshall Plan was one of the great initiatives of American diplomacy and certainly one of the most successful.

Later on that year, there was a second meeting of the Council of Foreign Ministers in London, where it was perfectly plain that the Soviets had no intention of permitting the unification of Germany. This was a matter of great concern to the Western Europeans. In fact, later on in December, Marshall had lunch with Ernest Bevin, who told him of his concern that Western Europe simply did not have the power to defend itself against the potential menace from the East, and what was the United States prepared to do about it? I was not present at the luncheon, but I heard afterwards from Marshall that what he had advised was the same formula that had been used in connection with the Marshall Plan; that is to say, the Europeans would come together for their own protection, see what they could do, and then turn to the United States and see what we could do to make up the difference between what the situation required and what they were able to do by their own efforts. This is the origin of the North Atlantic Treaty. The legislative basis for the treaty was laid down in a resolution adopted by the Senate on June 11, 1948, known as the Vandenburg Resolution (more properly, the Vandenburg-Lovett Resolution), which, in effect, authorized the United States to associate itself by constitutional process with regional and other collective arrangements based on self-help and mutual aid, permitted under Article 51 of the Charter of the United Nations .This resolution led to the signature on April 4, 1949, of the North Atlantic Treaty, the first military agreement which the United States had ever signed outside the Western Hemisphere. It is true that the Inter-American Treaty of Assistance was signed September 22, 1947, in Rio, and that a bilateral agreement on defense was signed with the Philippines in the same year. However, both of these had special justification. The first was merely giving more concrete form to the Monroe Doctrine; the case of the Philippines was an obvious continuation of the special relationship which had been in existence for many years. Article 5 of the North

Atlantic Treaty states that an attack on one could be an attack on all and that each member would then come to the assistance of the other with such means as it deemed feasible. Despite this rather empty qualification, it was clear that in the event of any attack on any member, the United States would almost automatically be at war. When the matter came up for consideration in the Senate, it was obvious that there were many Senators who were worried about this departure —from constitutional law, in the eyes of some; from isolationist tradition, to others. But finally they came along, somewhat reluctantly, and ratified the treaty, so that the United States from then on was really involved on a totally new course in its foreign policy.

It had come on us very suddenly. President Roosevelt died without any idea that the United States was going to be involved in military obligations in regard to the rest of the world. The treaty was followed later on in the 50s by a considerable number of other measures resulting largely from the war in Korea and the introduction of the SEATO arrangement for Southeast Asia, which was set up by the next administration. But the real period of change, the years of decision, were 1947 and 1948. In the Greek-Turkish scene, one of the phrases that President Truman used in presenting the measure to the Congress was that it should be the pol-

icy of the United States government to come to the
assistance of governments who were fighting against
armed minorities supported from abroad. The Marshall
Plan set the general pattern of economic assistance
which has been followed by the United States ever
since, and the North Atlantic Treaty set the pattern
to some extent for the treaties of mutual security
which we now have covering some 42 nations of the
world. We did this without pre-preparation by the
United States. It was not a planned operation. It was
not even a sought-after operation. It certainly was not
done in response to any material need of the United
States. The United States needed no more territory.
Economically it could assure its needs through the normal processes of trade. It was certainly not due to any
American ambition, nor any American wish. It was simply an American response to an external situation
which had developed as a result of the war. It was perfectly apparent that unless the United States took up
the challenge, a large part of the world would fall prey
to totalitarian power. There was an element of self-
interest in it, but I think also there was a good deal of
the element of the feeling of duty towards the civilized
world, as it then was. And one of the difficulties of
explaining this policy even in the early days, and even
more now, is that our policy is not rooted in any na-

tional material interest of the United States, as most foreign policies of other countries in the past have been. It is, for example, very difficult even now to say with great certainty what we do seek. We employ a number of generalities—a world of peace and a world free from threat, and a world that is suitable for commercial exchanges among other nations. These are vague and even banal statements. But as far as Europe was concerned, in 1949 when the treaty was adopted, it was fairly clear that there was a definite menace. It was clear then that Europe was divided as it is now. Europe was divided by the imposition of Communist regimes on all of Eastern Europe and on a third of Germany—and the city of Berlin was likewise split. In general all the consequences of this policy of ours were not fully anticipated by the government and only dimly perceived by the people of the United States.

In the transition from total protected isolationism, as the most secure—and non-military—country in the world, to the greatest responsibility that any single country has ever borne in the history of the world, we brought along a number of thought patterns which had grown up under isolationism. These thought patterns still exist and trouble our exercise or manipulation, if you will, of diplomacy. Thus, first of all, we have a tendency to regard foreign policy problems from a moral point of view, to see everything in black and white terms as good or bad. This approach tends to make the United States sometimes sound as though we are moralizing, adopting a holier-than-thou attitude which is excessively irritating to the more sophisticated nations. Secondly, we have a belief that any problem in international affairs is soluble; that with proper good will you can bring about a solution—and by that I mean a solution which will be regarded as permanent. In truth there is no such thing as a permanent solution in international affairs. There are only tolerable adjustments. And we believe rather excessively in the virtues of good will between nations. I must confess that one of the few things that I tend to agree with General de Gaulle on is his statement that nations are "cold monsters" devoid of sentiment, impervious to revenge, and guided by their own material interests. This is of course an overstatement of the case, particularly as far as the United States is concerned, but nevertheless I think one of the problems that we have in dealing with the European countries is that they tend to be impatient with what they would regard as the naïve sentimentality of Americans. Certainly in our dealings with the Soviet Union, we have seen how often the United States has been prepared to sacrifice precision for good will. It is not the best way of conducting

97

international affairs.

In the process which catapulted the United States from a position of total security into one of virtually total responsibility for large sections of the world, one of the inevitable results was a confrontation with the Soviet Union.

V

Soviet Nationalism—
Past, Present, and Future

I HAS OCCASIONALLY been said in criticism of American foreign policy that we have been too rigidly anti-Communist and that it was this exaggerated idea of the dangers of Communists that led the United States to become over-extended in the world. This criticism requires careful examination before it can be seriously entertained. If it is meant that during the period of Joseph McCarthy, the American government had a tendency to see Communism where it did not exist, there is some slight truth in the charge. But if it means that the United States was over-reacting to a real danger of a country falling under Communist domination, then it is without foundation. In the first place, to accuse the United States of anti-Communist sentiment is to ignore the fact that Communism, by its very nature, is deeply and permanently anti-American. In addition to general opposition to all systems of government which are not Soviet, the United States has been elected in the immediate postwar period to be Public Enemy Number One to the Communist movement all over the world. It should be emphasized that this anti-American element of Communism was proclaimed before the United States had taken any action to check the spread of Communism. Also, it must never be lost sight of that, despite the division in the Communist world, any new Communist country would automatically, by the very nature of things, become allied with the Soviet Union or, conceivably, with Communist China.* In the early 30s, we would have viewed with equal alarm the extension of the Fascist system allied with Nazi Germany as we now do the imposition of the Communist system allied with the Soviet Union. Both involve the balance of power in the world.

As I have noted, the Soviet government from the outset in November 1917 has exhibited a unique duality in all foreign-policy decisions. On the one hand there are the normal government-to-government relationships—relationships which have led throughout history to diplomacy. But in addition there is the revolutionary impulse (certainly somewhat more strongly

---

* The case of Yugoslavia was and is unique. It should not be forgotten that the United States, shortly after Tito had been ejected from the Communist fold, extended economic and subsequently military aid. Yugoslavia at that time still maintained her system and her fidelity to Communist doctrine.

present in the original Bolsheviki government than now). The duality was first made evident by Lenin in 1918, but it was Stalin who affirmed it and really created the Soviet Union as we know it today—its political structure and its consequent ideology. There is a definite and unbreakable connection between the political structure and the ideology of a country organized as is the Soviet Union. Stalin really had a strong nationalistic feeling for power, if you use the word *nationalistic* in terms of the Soviet regime, and not in the geographic sense of Russia the country. After he had really begun the process of industrialization of the Soviet Union and collectivization of its agriculture, Stalin moved to control the Comintern which had been set up by Lenin in 1919 as, I think, a genuine international revolutionary body to which all the Communist parties of the world were supposed to belong.

In Stalin's eyes, however, the Comintern and the Communist parties of the world were nothing but adjuncts to the Soviet power; he was essentially a cynic —with regard to normal affairs. He regarded the Communist parties as instruments to be totally and utterly subordinated to control from Moscow and by him personally. He purged the apparatus of the Comintern over and over again until he had an absolutely obedient instrument for his own purposes.

Revolution for revolution's sake was something for which he had little regard. He thought that revolution must be carefully organized and must be under the complete control of Moscow. There is in Vladimir Dedijer's book on Tito a report of a statement by Stalin on revolution, in which Stalin is quoted as having told the Chinese Communists that there was no point in trying to achieve a Communist victory in China.* He had advised them to go back to China and make the best peace they could with Chiang Kai-shek. Then, as Djilas wrote, Stalin complained that the Chinese Communists left Moscow and went back and did the exact opposite, which resulted in victory. This story is unquestionably true and reveals that Stalin did not expect or wish a Communist victory in China. First of all, he knew very well that if the Chinese Communists were in power they would have immense moral claims on the Soviets to help them. And secondly, it is very possible that Stalin, even at that time, 1948, foresaw some of the developments which have already occurred between China and the Soviet Union. Stalin communized Eastern Europe for two main reasons. One of them was security, and the other was ideology. Here was the happy circumstance in which the two important motivations of Soviet foreign policy coincided. But

* Vladimir Dedijer, *Tito,* Simon & Schuster, 1953.

Stalin was very reluctant to consider promoting a revolution that would be outside of the range of the Kremlin.

Therefore the explanation of Russian foreign policy, as we have seen it since the full flowering of the Stalin system could be called *Soviet* nationalism. I say *Soviet* rather than *Russian* because Soviet nationalism includes certain extensions brought on by ideology and goes beyond what would be the limits of Russian nationalism—Russian as pertaining to a geographical entity. This is the heritage from Stalin. The present rulers of Russia, an uneasy collective organization faced with signs of internal resentment, have inherited Stalin's system and follow in large measure his precepts.

An illustration of this is the military occupation of Czechoslovakia on August 20, 1968—a typical Stalinist move. The Soviets crushed the movement within the Czech Communist Party which, they felt, if allowed to continue, would lead to counter-revolution. This manifestation of Stalinism, distasteful as it is, reminds us of a certain fundamental Soviet principle: that is, to maintain, by any means whatever, the Soviet system in any contiguous state when this can be achieved without serious risk to the Soviet state itself. By the same token, the Soviets would be reluctant to consider the setting up of a Communist system which was not under

Moscow's direct control.

Soviet analysis of any foreign situation is not only conditioned by ideological considerations, it may be dominated by them. It is this factor that lies at the foundation of what we have come to call the cold war, which really started, insofar as the United States is concerned, in 1946, though we didn't acknowledge it until 1947. But, also, the ideological considerations have an effect on Soviet actions because of the great interest Soviet rulers have in the maintenance of their prestige in the Comunist world and their leadership over the Communist parties of the world. I have previously mentioned that the political structure of the Soviet Union as we know it today was really made by Stalin. It was created during the process of, and is in large measure of the consequence of, the attempt to industrialize a backward peasant country under forced draft. Industrialization gave rise to collectivization, because the Soviet government had to assure itself of control over the food supply in order to feed these new industrial complexes which they were planning to establish throughout the Soviet Union and particularly in western Siberia. Therefore, Soviet ideology was formed by the structure of the Soviet state, which resulted from a process of collectivization. But it was an ideology devoid of any vivifying factor. It was the expression of the bureaucratic mechanism of the structure that governed, and still governs, the Soviet Union. In spirit and content, Soviet ideology is far away from original Marxism and even original Leninism.

So great is the concern of the Soviet government over its leadership of the Communist world that in a number of cases one can detect a *purely* ideological basis for Soviet action. Take, for instance, Vietnam. The Soviet involvement in a massive program of military assistance to North Vietnam is entirely dictated by ideological considerations. Any other motivation does not stand examination. Consideration of power alone would certainly not have dictated the Soviet program of assistance to North Vietnam. The Soviet Union has, obviously no interest at present in helping the Chinese Communist government to increase its influence or authority in Southeast Asia. The simplest way to have avoided that happening would have been for the Soviets to have stayed out and let the North Vietnamese deal with the problems our involvement produced there for them. But had they done that, they would have lost prestige in the Communist world and along with it any pretension to leadership of the movement. They therefore decided, once we began to bomb North Vietnam, to go all out in furnishing military supplies, but *not* to run any risk of actual Soviet military involvement. They have been putting in on the average of a billion dollars a year—mostly in military supplies—to North Vietnam.

To touch on an important historical example of the nature of Soviet foreign policy: we see that when national and ideological considerations come into conflict, the national takes precedence. In the early days of the revolution, when the Soviet power was established in Moscow, the Comintern was initiated—largely under Lenin's influence in 1919—and Communist parties in opposition to those Socialist parties of the Second International were set up throughout the world. There was no possible conflict of material interest between the Communist party in any given country and the Soviet Union. The Kremlin's view on any international situation was absolutely dominant. This became particularly true in the era of Stalin, when he reduced the Communist parties to completely subservient factors. There was thus, for a number of years, not even the possibility of deviation between the Kremlin's attitude on an international situation and that of any other Communist party. There is one very clear illustration of this truth. The signing in 1939 of the Soviet Union's pact with Nazi Germany—and what this agreement meant—was a death blow not only to Communist policies in Europe but to the very existence of any

Communist party in Europe. Nevertheless, the Soviet Union did not hesitate. And in fact, even in the matter of peace with Germany in 1918, when it came to a conflict between Soviet national interests and ideology, it was always Soviet national interest that won out. Many more illustrations of this fact could be cited if space permitted.

Later on, following World War II, when a number of Communist regimes were instituted (or imposed, which is a more accurate word) by the Soviet Union through its army in Eastern Europe, then the objective setting came into being for a real test of one of the fundamental premises of Marxism and Leninism: that the dominant feature of human society was the reality of class warfare, and that nationalism and national differences between countries were secondary factors. According to the theory if there were ever established a system of Socialist states, the fact of their being Socialist would obliterate national differences. The first refutation of that theory came in 1948 when Tito resisted the attempts of the Soviet Union to put in instrumentalities of total control over the Yugoslav state. This led to the breach with Tito, and looking back on that period, one finds that the sharp edge of the cold war was turned against Tito the way it has been turned since 1946 against the United

States.

This was the first sign that the Marxian thesis of the secondary role of nationalism was subject, to put it mildly, to serious doubts. Stalin's solution was, of course, to excommunicate Tito, to mobilize all the forces—the imposing forces of the Kremlin propaganda mechanism—against Tito and his regime. But Stalin did not have recourse to military action such as was used in August 1968 against Czechoslovakia. One can only speculate on the reasons; it is never possible to be sure about the real reason for any given Soviet action. But certainly one of them was the feeling that an attack on Yugoslavia might easily have produced World War III. Also the Warsaw Pact was not in being and the Soviet Union did not have a common frontier with Yugoslavia.

Now in regard to the Soviet Union as a whole, what are the reasons that it has been a major source of preoccupation not only to the United States government but also to every government on the face of the earth, even including some of the satellite Soviet regimes in Eastern Europe? I think there are basically four reasons.

The first is the size of the country and its population. The Soviet Union has approximately 230 million people—a nation of extreme hardihood, tough, talented, and on the whole one of the foremost peoples of the world. Russia, long before the Soviet Union, had an impressive record of scientific personalities whose names were known all over the world. (One of them I might mention was Mendeleev, the man who first put together the Table of Elements.) The USSR covers one-sixth of the earth's surface and has within its confines all the resources needed to make a modern industrial state.

The second reason is that it is organized along totalitarian lines. And by totalitarian I mean just that word. Nazi Germany, despite the total dictatorship exercised by the Nazi party, despite its extreme brutality, nevertheless was not, in one sense of the word, a "totalitarian" state. There were entities in Germany which had been there before Hitler—banks, business institutions, publishing houses, press, all the media of the modern society; these were under the total control of Nazi Germany but were not changed. In the Soviet Union these same institutions, which existed before 1917, were dissolved, and indeed atomized by the Soviet government, which replaced any vestige of ownership with total ownership by the Soviet government. The government, in turn, was controlled by the Communist Party of the Soviet Union. Therefore, in a sense, the Soviet Union is the first totalitarian state the modern world has ever seen. All decisions in the Soviet Union are made by the eleven men who make up the political bureau of the Central Committee of the Communist Party of the Soviet Union. These are decisions that cover every phase of human life—political and economic; foreign policy, without question; military, social, information, cultural; every single detail of policy of any nature is controlled eventually by these eleven men.

The third reason, and one which is very actual today in view of the nature of the public discussion going on in the press, has to do with the military situation. The Soviet Union at no time since its inception in 1917 has ever relaxed its attention to its military posture or its military establishment.The rise of Soviet military power has been in one straight line from 1917 up to the present date. Of course at the end of the civil war in 1920 and after World War II there was some demobilization, but there never was any serious reduction of resources or effort applied to military development and related enterprises in the Soviet Union. Khrushchev indeed did cut back the land forces of the Soviet Union, much to the disgruntlement of the Soviet military, but he certainly increased the amount of funds devoted to missiles systems.

The fourth reason, which is the most difficult, the most slippery, is that of ideology. The Soviet Union came into power, and on the whole has lived by, an ideology one of whose fixed premises is that anything that is not Soviet is *ipso facto* inherently an enemy. The Soviet Union has never really departed from that. When they have had to make concessions to us, such as during the war, they speedily rectified them after the war with re-emergence of the fundamental premises of Marxism in a number of Soviet statements.

Those are the four reasons why the Soviet Union has been, and remains, a source of major preoccupation to any government in the world.

I now come to the current situation in the world and what the prospects for change are. The United States stands in a very different posture throughout the world than it did in 1929. As we know, the U.S. military budget jumped from less than a billion dollars (prewar) to (currently) eighty billion plus, and the State Department budget from less than fifteen million dollars to over four hundred fifty million. Whereas we had a single major international commitment in the Monroe Doctrine, we now have treaties with forty-two different countries either collectively or individually throughout the world, involving, in one form or another, possible military action in the event of an attack against any of the countries. We are a member, of course, and a very prominent member, of the United Nations, and a permanent member of the Security Council. All these make up a world that is very different in our point of view from what it was

25 or 30 years ago.

I cannot here go into the psychological changes that this shift produced in the United States. They obviously are very profound. But in regard to looking outward on the world, I will attempt to summarize how the world looks to the United States as I see it, in this year 1969.

First of all, Europe. I think one thing we must recognize is that our involvement, our participation, in the North Atlantic Treaty arrangement was entirely due to Soviet policy and power. Had the Soviet Union not chosen to prevent the unification of Germany in 1947 and 1948, there would have been no North Atlantic Treaty. It was a direct result of the division of Germany and of the consequent menace that most Europeans felt as a result. They felt the military weight of the Soviets very strongly and they turned to the United States with a request for us to supplement—or complement—their efforts at self-defense. This led to the North Atlantic Treaty, the first time in American history that the United States had entered into any military alliance with Europe since 1778.

The second event, and the one that pushed us into the Pacific, was the attack in Korea in 1950. Without that, I seriously doubt that we would have any involvements of a military nature in the Pacific—we might have, but on the whole it was certainly Korea that gave the impulse to it. It resulted in an agreement with Formosa and in an agreement with South Korea. There is one exception, the agreement that we had in 1946 with the Philippines; but this was a natural follow-up over the particular relations between the Philippines and the United States, as I have noted before, when they were given their independence in 1946. But apart from this treaty and the obligations of the Japanese occupation, we had no commitments in Asia. As a result of Korea, we not only had the individual treaties that I have mentioned with Formosa and with South Korea, but we also entered into the Southeast Asia Treaty Organization in 1954. And then, somewhat along that time, came the ANZUS treaties, which are at the moment not particularly operative but are manifestations of relationships between New Zealand, Australia, and the United States.

So, in effect, one can quite truthfully say that the United States policy in this field has always been in response to a Soviet action. A lot of people have criticized the United States for having too negative a policy or for always waiting for the other side to move before we act. But I don't think that is a very valid criticism. I think on the whole that this is rather a proof of the fact that we had no sinister design, no hidden purpose, certainly no imperialist ambitions, in our policy, but simply moved in answer to a challenge that was presented by the Soviet Union.

Now to the future. Looking at Europe, I see very little prospect of any change there. I believe—I hope and I believe—NATO will be maintained, because it seems to me that if there is any logic to be drawn from the events of summer 1968 in Czechoslovakia, it is that the Soviet Union, constructed as it is, is determined to keep Europe divided. And I say it is no secret that this dedication to division remains one of the most tricky and dangerous positions on the face of the globe. Divided countries in fact have been the chief military problem as far as the United States is concerned; and it is noteworthy that each one of these resulted from the imposition of a Communist regime in an area contiguous to a major Communist country. In Germany, it was the Soviet Union, clearly; in North Korea, it was the Soviet Union; in Vietnam, it was somewhat more complicated but the result is the same. The Communist area in each one of these countries has an inherent desire and interest in the unification of the country. The Communists have not done so in the case of Germany because the danger is much too great. Any move for unification of Germany by force from the East would result in World War III. We have made this plain; so have our Allies.

In Korea, we all know what happened when on June 25, 1950, the North Koreans attacked South Korea causing the involvement of the United States in the war, even though we had no treaty or obligation to do so. Vietnam is, as of this writing, uppermost in the minds of all Americans. I am not in a position to go into the matter, because I have no expert knowledge of the area at all, but I would merely like to point out that it is again the problem of a divided country.

The advantage, from a Communist point of view, of a divided country, and even the push for unification, is that the Communists can cloak themselves in the guise of champions of nationalism. This, to anybody who has really studied the Communist movement, is a secondary consideration to them, but nevertheless it affords a very excellent propaganda position from which to pursue this policy.

And let me add one thing here. While I know it is fairly popular now to regard Communism as somehow different than it has been (it is, some people say, no longer monolithic; "look at the Chinese-Soviet split"), nevertheless, Communism as a system still retains many of the same elements it has always had. A Communist frontier reminds me of what Friedrich Engels said about a military frontier; namely, that the difficulty with a military frontier is that anything that is 100 kilometers further out is preferable. And that statement applies literally to any Communist frontier. To any Communist system which is a closed society, where all information of any kind is controlled by the central authorities; any place where there is a common frontier with a country where there is freedom of expression or any of the customary freedoms that we know and understand is the point of danger for the Communists. There is a natural tendency for them to move that area of confrontation further away.

Therefore, looking at Europe, there seems to be little chance of any change in the situation as long as the structure of Communism and the Soviet Union remains unchanged.

The second point of possible danger is one that is very much in the public mind and on which our representatives in 1969 have met in New York with the Soviets, the French and the British, and that is the Middle East situation. Again, I am no expert on this part of the world, but it is perfectly clear that the whole problem evolved from the existence of Israel and the Arab-Israeli conflicts resulting from it. So strong are the emotions of hate and fear in that situation that it is very difficult to see exactly how the Middle East problem will work itself out. But one can find a certain element of encouragement in the fact that the four powers, supposedly the leading powers of the world—forgetting China for the moment —can meet on the subject; and I think they share one common purpose, and that is to see what can be done to prevent another open outbreak of warfare such as occurred in 1967 between the Israelis and the Arabs.

Turning to the Far East, it appears obvious that all events out there await the ultimate solution of the Vietnamese matter, which cannot be predicted. I think it is the most agonizing problem the United States has faced in a decade or more. And there does not seem to be anybody in the Nixon administration, any more than there was in the closing days of the Johnson administration, who has any clear idea exactly how it is going to end.

But that is the way the world looks, as far as one can see it at the present moment. I would like to close this book on the discussion of what the possibilities of change in the Soviet structure seem to be, because this is the key to a great deal. I have not discussed the Chinese-Soviet relations, which perhaps, in Soviet eyes, are most important of all, but to add a few words on this subject: the Chinese-Soviet dispute, in conspicuous terms, began at least ten years ago. Originally it was ideological because the Chinese, being the last to receive the "benefits" of a Communist system, had a tendency to take the sacred literature of Marx rather literally. They appear to have really believed that, if they became Communist they would be treated by the leading Communist country as though they were part of that country, and that, therefore, the Soviet Union would give aid freely, and without conditions, to the Communist Chinese. The Soviets would share their nuclear secrets with the Chinese and in general would act as though there were no geographical difference between the two countries. This turned out to be totally wrong. As events developed in the late 1950s and early 1960s, the Chinese became completely disillusioned because the Soviets never had any idea of treating the Chinese in this manner. In 1960 the Soviet Union suddenly withdrew their technicians and ended even their modest nuclear cooperation.

The result is a split in the Communist world, and this is one of the reasons the Soviet Union took so much effort in 1969 to bring together 75 of the 88 Communist parties in the world in Moscow—to line them up with the Soviet Union and not with the Chinese. The propaganda is very bitter—Soviet propaganda against Mao is equal to, if not surpassing, the bitterness and the venom of cold war expressions which were directed at us, particularly during the Korean War. The Soviet Union finds itself confronted with a very serious dilemma at the present time. The country is run by the Communist Party, which, I have always believed, was conceived by Lenin primarily as a revolutionary instrument, not essentially as a governing mechanism. It only became an actual and general governing mechanism under Stalin. In Lenin's day the

Party was the ultimate source of power, but the mechanism through which this power was implemented was not so much the Communist Party as the Soviet system. Under Stalin, following industrialization and the purges, the Party was placed in total and operational command of all phases of Soviet life. A government structure exists parallel with the Party structure at all levels but entirely subordinate to the Party. The leaders of the Party are the guardians of the ideology— they are also its prisoners. The whole bureaucratic structure is dependent upon ideology to maintain it; ideology is the cement that holds the whole structure together; but it is visibly not the kind of structure that is capable of dealing effectively and smoothly with the requirements of a modern industrial civilization. I feel, as I have said, though I would not venture to predict how long it is going to take, that sooner or later there is bound to be a change in this unnatural organization of human society. And when it does change, there are going to be all sorts of very interesting developments in the Soviet Union. The Soviet Union is really an empire. In Communist philosophy, an empire is usually one where you cross water in order to impose your system. The Russians have done it by absorbing contiguous territories. But this does not obviate the fact that there are many nationalities within the confines of the Soviet Union. If there is a breakup of the Party control—which in a sense is a canny concealment of the dominance by a Slavic majority over other peoples in the Soviet Union—we can expect a re-emergence of national sentiment among the subject peoples. I venture no prediction as to timing or as to how it will happen. It could take the form of a *coup d'état,* conceivably a move by the military to assert themselves. I don't believe that there will ever be a mass revolt and a rebellion in the true sense of the word. Some form of palace *coup d'état* seems more likely. Until this happens, there appears to be very little possibility that the United States will be relieved of the burdens which it assumed in the late 1940s and early 1950s. I see very little chance that our military budget will be very much smaller. I see no chance of the United States' being able to return to the more tranquil days of prewar when we were protected and secure. I think we are in the world, and I do not think that we are going to be able to withdraw from it. It seems to me that the task for us is to try and live with the problem which the world presents to us, and do it in such a way that we do not falter or slip in the tasks that we have assumed.

I know very well that the military installation of the United States presents a great problem to our people. In fact, the first one who spoke of the problem of military establishment in a democracy on this continent was George Washington in his farewell address to the American people. He said, "They no longer have the necessity of those overgrown military establishments which under any form of government are inauspicious to liberty, and which are to be regarded as particularly hostile to republican liberty." Thus George Washington in September 1796.

Of course—and I write now from my wartime personal experience—the war was necessarily run by the military, a natural circumstance, but always under the control of the civilian authority. In my forty years as a Foreign Service officer of the United States, I can think of no single decision that has ever been taken by the American military contrary to the wishes of the constituted civilian authority. All the mistakes we made —and indeed we have made them—have been made by the civilian authorities. I have had the pleasure of knowing a number of our top military, and those who had—or have—any dangerous potential for American democracy can be counted on the fingers of one hand. But this is not the point. The present and future point is that any element of society, any group, given eighty billion dollars to spend in the American economy becomes a major factor—one to be reckoned with by both the Congress and the people of the United States.

In this brief account I have sought to trace the

course of events which led to the transformation of the United States from a safe, protected country, unhampered by involvement in world affairs, into one having many obligations and vast responsibilities in the world. I do not assert that the policy of the United States has been perfect by any means. It can be said, and possibly correctly, that the United States overextended itself and that it had been overzealous in some of its commitments. The record, however, may well bear the scrutiny of critics, and the history of this period in which the United States rose to meet a challenge which had no origin or roots within our country, and to adopt a policy not dictated by any American material need and certainly not in response to any American ambition or desire, is not one of which we should be ashamed. It is to be hoped that the obvious, understandable anguish and dismay, and even anger over the apparently unsoluble difficulties and horrors we are encountering in Vietnam will not serve to discolor or darken the picture as a whole. One thing, however, is clear: there is no return to the comfortable isolation of the past. The United States is in the world and cannot avoid the responsibilities—except at its peril—which history has placed on its shoulders as the strongest power on earth.

Index